I0053645

Data Rookies:
Data Mining Basics

Discover Patterns and Insights

Published by
Data Analytics Curriculum
https://www.dataanalyticscurriculum.com

Supplements and Companion Books

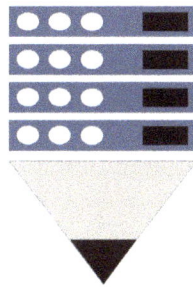

Data Analytics Curriculum

Data Analytics Curriculum, LLC develops approachable and visually engaging educational materials designed to make data science and technology accessible to learners ranging from high school through college and independent study.

The content texts, such as this book, are sold separately from the lab and exercise books because they can be paired with multiple technologies.

This book has accompanying lab exercise books available for R (coding-based) and Orange (non-coding-based), with plans to add more technologies in the future.

For additional titles, lab books, solution guides, slides, and other teaching and learning resources, please visit our store or website:

Website: https://www.dataanalyticscurriculum.com

Contents

Contents

Chapter 1

Foundations of Data Mining

Welcome! In this chapter we'll delve into the essence of data mining and cover some fundamental aspects. Our primary goal is to articulate what data mining entails and set the stage for further study.

Data mining can be defined in a few ways depending on the perspective. Firstly, data mining can be viewed as a process. From this angle, data mining is akin to a search for patterns within a dataset. Whether consumer data revealing purchasing behaviors or medical data unveiling disease-symptom correlations, the essence remains the same: identifying patterns within data. This perspective emphasizes the core aspect of data mining—uncovering meaningful patterns. In essence, data mining mirrors the process of mining for gold, where the objective is to extract valuable insights from a vast expanse of data.

Academically, data mining is an interdisciplinary field that employs techniques from mathematics, statistics, computer science (including database management and programming), and machine learning/artificial intelligence, along with domain-specific knowledge from fields like business and healthcare. Contrary to popular belief, data mining isn't solely a realm of mathematics or computer science. To set the stage for this book, it's crucial to understand that much like data analytics itself, data mining uses techniques from many academic disciplines.

1-1 History of data mining

To understand the history of data mining, it's essential to recognize that it's not entirely a novel field and has evolved over decades. Data mining has roots that stretch back quite a while, though not in the context we typically associate with it today. Let's review some key highlights to provide perspective on its evolution.

The origins of data mining can be traced back to the 1960s. Early computing machines, though primitive by today's standards, hinted at the potential for automating analytical tasks. Before this period, data management primarily relied on manual processes, with information stored in physical documents within office settings.

However, the landscape began to shift in the 1970s, marking the initial steps towards what we now recognize as data mining. As we moved into the 1970s, there was a gradual shift towards computerized data management. While still in its infancy, the concept of automating analytical processes became increasingly feasible with the emergence of rudimentary computing technology.

By the 1980s, data mining began to take shape as a defined practice. Desktop computers became increasingly prevalent. Shapiro, in the late '80s, introduced the concept of "knowledge discovery in databases" (KDD), which essentially encompasses what we now know as data mining. Despite the term "data mining" being coined earlier by Fedman, KDD became synonymous with the process of uncovering patterns and relations within data.

The 1990s witnessed a proliferation of computer usage, with desktop computers becoming commonplace. While internet usage was still in its nascent stages, the widespread adoption of desktop computers laid the groundwork for the digital age to come. Alongside this technological boom, businesses began to recognize the value of leveraging data for profit. In a capitalist society like America, where value and profit are paramount, the importance of data surged.

As businesses embraced data-driven decision-making, the late '90s and early 2000s witnessed a surge in interest and investment in data analytics. With the proliferation of internet usage, businesses recognized the potential of data to uncover valuable insights, particularly in areas such as sales and customer behavior analysis.

In essence, the 1990s marked a turning point where the convergence of technology, business needs, and academic research propelled data mining into the forefront of innovation and profitability.

Moving into the 2000s, coinciding with the internet boom, there was a notable emergence of open-source data mining tools, exemplified by the advent of R, a freely available platform. The accessibility of such tools democratized data analysis, driving increased adoption due to their cost-effectiveness. The early 2000s saw the publication of seminal works in data mining, such as a prominent textbook released in 2003. These resources played a pivotal role in the proliferation of data mining courses and the subsequent expansion of the field.

Moreover, the concept of "Big Data" gained traction during this period, reflecting the exponential growth in data volume facilitated by the internet explosion. While the term lacks a precise definition, it underscores the unprecedented scale of data collection and the challenges and opportunities it presents for analysis and utilization. Technological advancements also played a crucial role, with platforms like Apache Hadoop simplifying the storage and processing of large datasets. This development marked a significant milestone in handling the burgeoning volumes of data generated in the digital age.

As we entered the 2010s, cloud computing emerged as a transformative force. This shift from local server-based infrastructure to cloud-based data storage revolutionized data management practices. The advent of cloud computing facilitated the creation of vast data warehouses, housed in secure facilities known as the "cloud." This shift paved the way for unprecedented scalability and accessibility of data resources.

The early 2010s witnessed a remarkable surge in machine learning and artificial intelligence (AI) technologies. The rise of social media platforms like Facebook further fueled the demand for data analysis tools. However, this period also saw controversies surrounding data privacy and collection practices, exemplified by incidents involving Facebook.

In 2011, IBM showcased the capabilities of AI through its computer Watson, which famously competed on Jeopardy. This demonstration highlighted the power of machine learning and natural language processing in solving complex tasks. Additionally, Google's release of TensorFlow in 2012 marked a significant milestone in open-source machine learning libraries. TensorFlow quickly emerged as one of the most widely used tools in the field, reflecting its versatility and effectiveness in various applications.

The midpoint of the decade saw the emergence of deep learning as a dominant paradigm in AI research. This sophisticated approach to machine learning, characterized by hierarchical layers of neural networks, revolutionized various domains, including computer vision and natural language processing.

A significant breakthrough occurred in 2019 with the release of language models for natural language processing. Unlike computer languages with fixed meanings, natural language presents challenges due to its semantic complexities. This development enabled computers to comprehend contextual nuances, paving the way for innovations like chatbots and AI applications.

Cloud computing has streamlined data access and analysis for businesses by decentralizing data storage and enabling remote access via the internet. Consequently, the 2010s and 2020s have witnessed the evolution and expansion of data mining, with continuous advancements in techniques and tools. While data mining lays the groundwork for artificial intelligence, the latter encompasses broader domains like natural language processing and other computational aspects.

However, with progress comes responsibility. The 2020s have brought heightened awareness of privacy concerns and ethical considerations surrounding data usage. As data analytics professionals, it's crucial to navigate these issues ethically and responsibly.

Review Questions

1. How was data handled before the 1960s?
2. What is KDD and who introduced it?
3. How did desktop computers help data mining grow?
4. Why was the 1990s a turning point for data mining?
5. What impact did open-source tools like R have?
6. How did cloud computing change data analysis?
7. What was the significance of TensorFlow in 2012?
8. What happened in 2019 that advanced language AI?

1-2 Types of data

Learning Outcomes

1-2-1 Identify common types of data used in analytics.
1-2-2 State the differences between structured and unstructured data.
1-2-3 Give real-world examples of various data types.
1-2-4 Explain why different data types require different analysis approaches.

Data has many different types.

Types of Data

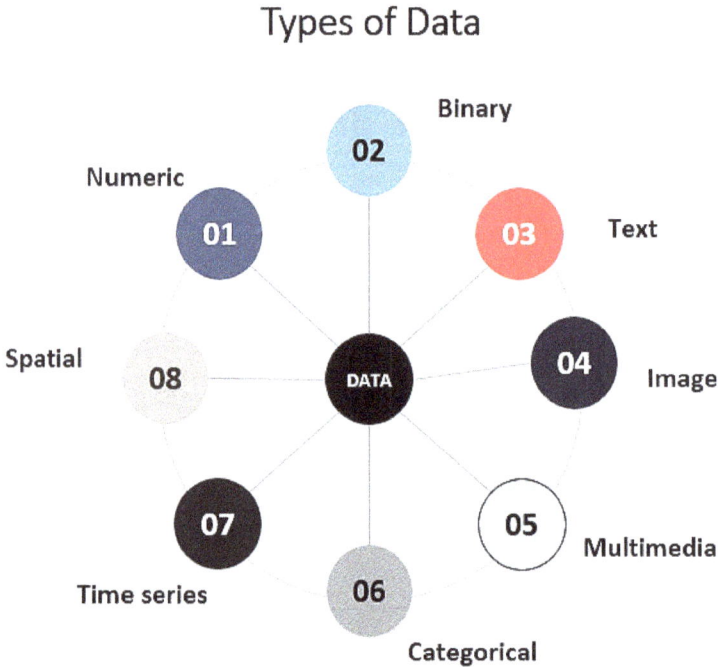

First, there's numeric data, which aligns with what's typically encountered in introductory statistics classes. Numeric data lends itself well to analysis using basic statistical methods. However, it's important to note that data analytics, including data mining, encompasses more than just numerical data.

Binary data, for instance, traces back to the fundamental language of computers, comprised of zeros and ones. This form of data underpins the digital world, functioning at the most elemental level of computing processes.

Text data represents another significant category, often referred to as unstructured data. This includes a vast array of information found in textual formats, such as social media posts, emails, and documents. Analyzing text data presents unique challenges due to its unstructured nature, but advancements in computational capabilities have opened new avenues for extracting insights from this rich source of information.

Image data is also considered unstructured data. Audio data is another type of unstructured data, representing sound and speech. Video and movie data combine both image and audio data and are similarly categorized as unstructured data.

Categorical data, on the other hand, encompasses discrete, qualitative information, like colors, genders, or species. While not as lengthy as textual data, categorical data provides valuable insights into various attributes and characteristics.

Time series data is another essential type, capturing observations collected over sequential intervals. This data is crucial in analyzing trends and patterns over time, particularly in domains such as sales forecasting and economic analysis.

Spatial data is another significant type of data, which is commonly used in mapping the Earth. Organizations like the UN have been heavily involved in this field. Although most of the Earth's surface has likely been mapped using GPS coordinates, spatial data still plays a crucial role in geographic and environmental studies

Each type of data presents its own set of challenges and opportunities for analysis. Understanding these distinctions is essential for effectively leveraging data analytics techniques to derive actionable insights. Techniques of data mining can be applied to all kinds of data.

Review Questions

1. How do numeric and categorical data differ?
2. Why is text data unstructured, and what makes it hard to analyze?
3. How is spatial data used? Give an example.
4. How are audio and video different from structured data?
5. When is time series data useful, and what can it show?

1-3 Data mining process

Learning Outcomes

1-3-1 Outline the 5 steps of the data mining process.
1-3-2 Explain the role of data preparation and exploration.

The data mining process we're following is inspired by the CRISP-DM (Cross-Industry Standard Process for Data Mining) methodology. While CRISP-DM provides a specific algorithm for data mining, it is adapted and modified slightly here. The general pattern remains the same, though the specifics may vary slightly.

Here's an overview of our data mining process, represented as a staircase with five steps:

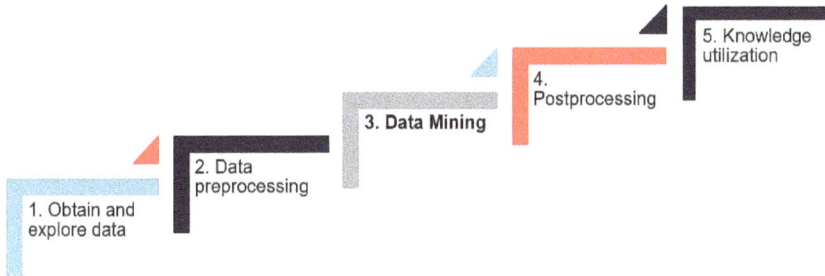

Step 1: Obtain and explore data

The initial phase involves gathering and examining the data. Typically, data comes from a database or data warehouse system maintained by IT professionals. An analyst will either receive the data from IT or retrieve it directly using SQL or related technology. Once the data is obtained, the analyst uploads it into the software tool they will use for analysis. This tool may be the same for all steps of the data mining process or different software may be used for different tasks.

During this phase, the data should be thoroughly explored to understand its structure and contents. This includes generating summaries such as frequency distributions, creating visualizations, and analyzing variables to gain a comprehensive understanding of the dataset.

Step 2: Data preprocessing

This step involves cleaning and transforming the data to prepare it for analysis. Essential pre-processing tasks include modifying data, handling missing values, and other necessary preparations. Pre-processing is crucial for ensuring that the data is suitable for data mining and may involve several activities:

- Cleaning/Reformatting/Transforming Data: Adjusting data formats, correcting errors, and converting data into a suitable format for analysis.

- Reducing Dimensionality: Simplifying the dataset by reducing the number of variables while retaining essential information.

- Filtering/Subsetting Data: Selecting specific subsets of data that are relevant to the analysis.

- Normalizing Data: Adjusting data values to a common scale to ensure consistency and improve the performance of data mining algorithms.

Step 3: Data mining

The core focus of this book lies here. This step involves applying clustering, association, and classification techniques to find patterns in the data.

Step 4: Postprocessing

In this phase, we evaluate the effectiveness of the models created during data mining, particularly classification models. Post-processing involves several key steps:

- Assess Model Performance- You'll learn how to evaluate the performance of your models using various metrics and techniques.

- Validate the Model- Ensure that the model is both sensible and effective by checking its accuracy and relevance.

- Make Adjustments- Based on the evaluation, make any necessary adjustments to improve the model's performance.

The goal of post-processing is to ensure that the models are reliable and can provide meaningful insights.

Step 5: Application of Knowledge

This step involves using the insights gained from data mining to make informed decisions or solve specific problems. The knowledge derived, often in the form of a new model, is applied for practical and productive purposes. This may include:

- Implementing Solutions: Applying the model to real-world scenarios to address specific issues or improve processes.

- Informed Decision-Making: Using the insights to guide strategic decisions and optimize outcomes.

- Continuous Improvement: Leveraging the model to continually enhance business operations, customer experiences, or other targeted areas.

Review Questions

1. What are the five steps in the data mining process?
2. Why is data cleaning important?
3. Name two preprocessing techniques.
4. What are common data mining methods?
5. How do you evaluate a model?
6. How can mining results be used in practice?

1-4 Case study

Consider an example where a bank wants to be able to predict mortgage approvals based on several factors, such as employment history and down payment. Let's walk through the five steps outlined above using this example. This dataset is simplified for illustration purposes. Typically, your dataset would be much larger.

Step 1: Obtain and explore data

The first thing after obtaining the data is to understand the relevant variables and explore the data. The data includes variables like credit score, income, employment history, debt-to-income ratio, loan-to-value ratio, property type, down payment, loan purpose, and approval status.

Credit Score	Income	Employment History (years)	Debt-to-Income Ratio	Loan-to-Value Ratio	Property Type	Down Payment	Purpose	Approval
700	60000	3	0.4	0.8	Single-Family	20000	Primary Residence	Approved
650	80000	5	0.3	0.75	Condo	15000	Vacation Home	Approved
600	40000	2	0.6	0.95	Multi-Unit	10000	Investment Property	Denied
720	90000	8	0.2	0.6	Single-Family	50000	Primary Residence	Approved
620	55000	4	0.5	0.9	Single-Family	30000	Primary Residence	Denied
680	70000	6	0.35	0.85	Condo	20000	Vacation Home	Appr

Even if you're not trained in mortgages, these variables are understandable to most educated people. For example, credit score reflects creditworthiness, income shows how much the applicant earns, employment history indicates job stability, and the debt-to-income ratio compares debt to income (which likely includes the mortgage). Basic exploratory data analysis on the data should be performed (frequency tables, summary statistics) to be familiar with the data before further analysis.

Step 2: Data preprocessing

Preprocessing is the step where you prepare data for mining. Cleaning, transforming, and manipulating data are essential skills referred to as data wrangling (a subject in and of itself). Before applying data mining techniques, you commonly will need to reduce the dimensionality of your data, filter or subset it, normalize it, and convert it to a standard scale to remove the units, which can interfere with analysis.

Because credit scores can be on different scales (different credit rating agencies) this data needs to be normalized (to a standard normal score). Some cleaning of the data is performed as well to make the approved data column consistent.

Credit Score	Normalized credit score	Income	Employment History (years)	Debt-to-Income Ratio	Loan-to-Value Ratio	Property Type	Down Payment	Purpose	Approval
700	2	60000	3	0.4	0.8	Single-Family	20000	Primary Residence	Approved
650	1.5	80000	5	0.3	0.75	Condo	15000	Vacation Home	Approved
600	1	40000	2	0.6	0.95	Multi-Unit	10000	Investment Property	Denied
720	2.2	90000	8	0.2	0.6	Single-Family	50000	Primary Residence	Approved
620	1.2	55000	4	0.5	0.9	Single-Family	30000	Primary Residence	Denied
680	1.8	70000	6	0.35	0.85	Condo	20000	Vacation Home	Approved

Step 3. Data Mining

After pre-processing, the data is ready to apply various data mining techniques. The technique to use depends on the data and goals of analysis. Because the goal in this example is to predict loan approval/denial (a binary outcome) a linear discrimination analysis method or logistic regression would be an appropriate data mining technique here.

To build this model, you take your input variables (excluding the last column, which is your labeled outcome) and create a predictive model with loan approval as the output. The goal is to determine which variables are most important in predicting loan approval.

When you look at the data, you might notice patterns. Data mining is all about finding these patterns. For example, low credit scores and high loan-to-value ratios are often not good indicators for mortgage approval. This pattern recognition is the essence of data mining: analyzing data to find useful patterns. If you worked in a bank, you could use these patterns to develop a model for predicting mortgage approvals.

It is likely from looking at the patterns in the data that the normalized credit score and loan to value ratio would be specific predictors in the model (note this example is too small to run this data and presented for conceptual purposes).

Credit Score	Normalized credit score	Income	Employment History (years)	Debt-to-Income Ratio	Loan-to-Value Ratio	Property Type	Down Payment	Purpose	Approval
700	2	60000	3	0.4	0.8	Single-Family	20000	Primary Residence	Approved
650	1.5	80000	5	0.3	0.75	Condo	15000	Vacation Home	Approved
600	1	40000	2	0.6	0.95	Multi-Unit	10000	Investment Property	Denied
720	2.2	90000	8	0.2	0.6	Single-Family	50000	Primary Residence	Approved
620	1.2	55000	4	0.5	0.9	Single-Family	30000	Primary Residence	Denied
680	1.8	70000	6	0.35	0.85	Condo	20000	Vacation Home	Approved

Step 4: Postprocessing

After building your model, you enter the post-processing phase, where you evaluate its effectiveness. You need to determine if the model is sensible and effective.

To ensure the model's reliability, the bank might test it with additional data ('test' data) not used in making the model ('training' data) to make sure the model is accurately predicting. This process involves splitting a larger dataset into training and testing sets. You build the model with the training set and then test it with the testing set. This helps validate the model's effectiveness, which is an essential part of postprocessing.

Step 5: Application of Knowledge

After a model is made and the model is sensible and proven accurate through postprocess testing it can then be used. In the case of mortgages, the model would be used to approve or deny loans.

1-5 Tools

There are many software tools used in data mining, encompassing various applications and programs. While technology evolves over time, the underlying theory of data mining remains constant. This is why this book isn't tied to any specific software. The theoretical foundations you will learn will stay relevant, even as you encounter new tools and technologies.

Data mining tools can be broadly categorized into several types, each serving different aspects of the data mining process.

Tools

PROGRAMMING LANGUAGES   **1**

2   SPECIALIZED SOFTWARE.

GENERAL SOFTWARE   **3**

4   BUSINESS INTELLIGENCE

STATISTICAL SOFWARE   **5**

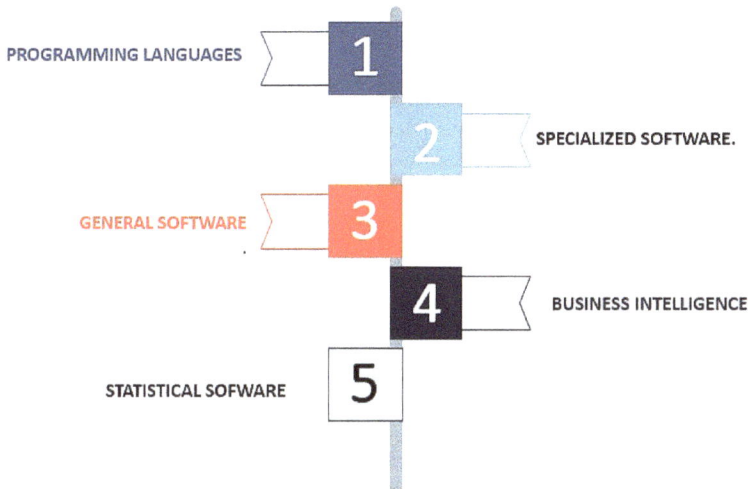

Firstly, there's general-purpose software like Microsoft Excel and Google Sheets. While these aren't dedicated to data mining tools, they offer limited data mining capabilities. For example, Excel has plugins such as XL Miner, though its functionality is somewhat restricted. Despite this, Excel and Google Sheets are useful for basic data manipulation and cleaning tasks, which are essential components of data wrangling.

Next, we have statistical software, including tools like SPSS (IBM), SAS, and Minitab. While these have been available longer than dedicated data mining tools, they integrate some data mining functionality. However, they are primarily proprietary and may have costly licenses. SAS is recognized for its high cost, while SPSS is frequently utilized in academic disciplines such as psychology and social sciences. Mastering these tools effectively can be challenging due to their complexity.

Another noteworthy category of tools is data visualization and business intelligence (BI) tools. Examples include Tableau and Power BI, which excel at swiftly and effectively presenting data for insights. However, their emphasis is usually on visualization rather than specific data mining algorithms. While Tableau is esteemed for its visualization capabilities, Power BI has constraints, especially for Macintosh users, rendering it less accessible.

In addition to these tools, programming languages such as Python and R play a crucial role in data mining. R offers robust capabilities for data manipulation, analysis, and modeling, making it a favored choice among data scientists and analysts. Proficiency in programming languages like R and Python unlocks opportunities for more customized and advanced analytics tasks. However, the level of programming expertise needed varies depending on the specific role and industry. For example, advanced data science roles may require more extensive programming knowledge compared to applied analytics roles, where programming skills may be less critical. SQL also plays a significant role in data mining for data wrangling and retrieving data from databases.

Another excellent choice for data mining is specialized software like Orange, an open-source tool that operates on Python but provides a user-friendly visual programming interface. Although it functions on Python in the background, you aren't required to directly code in Python to utilize it. Orange has a longstanding history of over two decades and enjoys widespread adoption in research, biology, and medical sectors. Without directly writing Python code, utilizing Orange allows you to focus on the analytical work and not the programming.

Review Questions

1. Why does this book focus on theory rather than specific software?
2. What are some limits of using Excel or Google Sheets for data mining?
3. How do SPSS and SAS differ from tools like Orange?
4. What is the primary focus of BI tools like Tableau and Power BI?
5. Why are R and Python important in data mining?
6. What makes Orange a good tool for beginners?

1-6 Ethics and limitation

Learning Outcomes

1-6-1 Understand key ethical issues in data mining.

1-6-2 Recognize limitations due to non-random, biased data.

1-6-3 Compare data mining with traditional statistical methods.

1-6-4 Identify risks of biased algorithms in real-world decisions.

1-6-5 Appreciate the need for ethical responsibility in analytics.

1-6-6 Understand that legal standards for data use are evolving.

Ethical considerations in data mining are of paramount importance. As data mining becomes increasingly integrated into business, healthcare, education, government, and other sectors, understanding its ethical dimensions is not optional—it is essential. Unlike traditional statistics, which often operate on data obtained through carefully designed research studies using random sampling and controlled environments, data mining frequently deals with vast, unstructured, and non-random datasets. These datasets are often collected for convenience rather than scientific rigor, potentially introducing biases that can skew results and lead to misleading or even harmful outcomes.

Data mining is primarily exploratory rather than experimental. It is not driven by hypotheses in the way formal statistical testing is. Instead, it seeks to uncover patterns, trends, and relationships in large datasets, often without a clear sense of what will be found. This exploratory nature presents unique limitations. While it can lead to valuable insights, it also increases the risk of false patterns—correlations that appear meaningful but are the result of chance or underlying biases. Without appropriate safeguards and critical thinking, it is easy to mistake noise for signal.

The design and approach of data mining differ significantly from traditional statistical methods. Statistical analysis often involves well-established structures such as treatment and control groups, designed experiments, and clearly defined variables. In contrast, data mining emphasizes flexibility and adaptability. Its goal is to discover hidden patterns, not necessarily to confirm or reject a hypothesis. This flexibility, while powerful, also demands ethical responsibility. Practitioners must be aware that they are not working within a neutral or objective system—biases in the data, the tools, and even in human interpretation can all influence outcomes.

One of the most significant limitations of data mining lies in the nature of the data itself. Convenience sampling—where data is collected simply because it is easy or readily available—can result in unrepresentative datasets. For instance, web and social media data typically reflect the behavior of specific groups with access to the internet, skewing younger, wealthier, and more educated. Using such data to draw conclusions about broader populations can result in misinformed decisions and policies.

Moreover, the legal and ethical implications of data usage are continually evolving. Issues such as privacy, consent, data ownership, and algorithmic transparency are at the forefront of modern data ethics. Regulatory frameworks like the General Data Protection Regulation (GDPR) in Europe and the California Consumer Privacy Act (CCPA) in the United States attempt to address these concerns, but the pace of technological change often outstrips legal oversight.

A particularly critical ethical issue arises when data mining is used to develop predictive algorithms that influence real-world decisions—such as mortgage approvals, job screenings, medical diagnoses, or policing practices. These algorithms can inadvertently perpetuate existing societal biases if the data they are trained on reflect historical inequities. For example, a mortgage approval algorithm trained on historical data may deny loans to applicants from certain racial or socioeconomic groups if those groups were historically underserved or discriminated against. In such cases, biased data can lead directly to discriminatory outcomes, despite the lack of explicit intent.

Therefore, ethical vigilance is essential throughout the entire data mining process. Analysts must ask difficult questions: *Where did this data come from? Who does it include—and who does it leave out? Are the patterns we're seeing truly meaningful, or are they artifacts of biased data?* Transparency in methodology, fairness in algorithmic design, and accountability in decision-making are not just technical best practices—they are ethical imperatives.

As students and practitioners of data mining, it is crucial to move beyond the technical aspects of the field and embrace an ethical mindset. As we explore tools and techniques in the chapters ahead, we must also remain aware of the broader impacts of our work. Ethics is not a side note in data mining— it is a foundational element that ensures our analyses are responsible, fair, and ultimately beneficial to society.

Example

Predictive Policing and Ethical Pitfalls

A city police department decides to implement a data mining system to identify neighborhoods where crimes are likely to occur. The algorithm uses historical crime data to predict hot spotsthat warrant increased police presence. Initially, the program appears to be successful—it identifies areas with frequent past incidents, and patrols are dispatched accordingly.

However, upon closer examination, a troubling pattern emerges. The historical data used to train the model was not neutral; it reflected decades of biased policing practices. Minority neighborhoods had been disproportionately policed in the past, leading to higher recorded crime rates—not necessarily because more crimes were committed there, but because there was more surveillance and reporting in those areas.

As a result, the predictive policing algorithm reinforces this bias. It continues to send more police to the same neighborhoods, increasing surveillance and arrests. Meanwhile, under-policed areas, where crimes are underreported, receive little attention, even though they may have similar or greater need for intervention.

This cycle creates a feedback loop: biased data leads to biased predictions, which leads to more biased data collection. Residents of over-policed neighborhoods experience increased scrutiny and tension, while broader social issues go unaddressed.

This example highlights several key ethical issues:

Bias in data collection (historical inequities),

Lack of representativeness (ignoring under-policed areas),

Algorithmic opacity (the model's decision-making process is not transparent),

Impact on vulnerable communities (reinforcing systemic injustice),

Accountability (no one is clearly responsible for the outcomes).

Only by questioning the origins of the data, validating the fairness of the algorithm, and involving community stakeholders could the project be redesigned to serve all citizens more equitably.

Review Questions

1. How does data mining differ from traditional statistics in its design?
2. Why is non-random data a limitation in data mining?
3. Give an example of how bias can enter a data mining project.
4. Why are ethical concerns important when creating algorithms?
5. What kinds of decisions can be affected by biased data?
6. How are legal and ethical standards for data use changing?

Chapter 2

Obtaining and Exploring Data

Data mining follows a step-by-step paradigm, starting with obtaining and exploring data. That's where this chapter begins.

1. Obtain and explore data

2-1 Obtaining Data

Learning Outcomes

2-1-1 List ways to get data.

2-1-2 Know why CSV files are useful.

2-1-3 Spot messy or confusing data.

2-1-4 Tell the difference between structured and unstructured data.

2-1-5 Understand that data can be biased.

Data source

Data can originate from diverse origins. In the past, prior to the rise of cloud computing and widespread internet connectivity, computers operated largely in isolation. Data was stored locally on floppy disks or hard drives, and if data exchange was necessary, it was commonly facilitated by physical mailing disks.

In contemporary times, data acquisition often involves linking to a database. This connection could entail retrieving data either through internet access or within a company's internal network. In the latter scenario, you might establish a connection to another computer within the company via an internal network, bypassing the internet, to access a backend database.

When establishing a connection to a database, the standard protocol employed is Open Database Connectivity (ODBC), offering a uniform method for connecting to and engaging with databases. Structured Query Language (SQL) serves as the primary means to query data, facilitating tasks such as selecting specific data from tables.

Alternatively, you may opt to extract data from the internet through web scraping, albeit with accompanying considerations and constraints. The legal ambiguity surrounding web scraping underscores the necessity to comprehend the legal and ethical ramifications before engaging in such activities.

Moreover, data can originate from a myriad of sources, encompassing automated data collection by machines, customer transactions conducted in brick-and-mortar stores, and diverse business networks. Numerous businesses engage in ongoing data collection across various operations.

Conversely, manual data entry may still be necessary, particularly in instances involving research or data collection during site visits. However, this manual process can be laborious and time-consuming.

File types

When it comes to file types, data can be stored in a variety of formats. If your goal is to analyze data, strive to obtain CSV (comma-separated values) files whenever feasible, as they tend to be the most universally compatible for reading and writing across different software systems, including R and Excel.

Proprietary file formats, such as those utilized by SAS and SPSS, are prevalent in high-end software requiring expensive licenses. While SAS is widely utilized, it's advisable to avoid receiving data in SAS formats if you lack access to the respective software. Even with programming code to manage these formats, ensuring correct formatting can pose challenges. Therefore, opting for a straightforward file type like CSV is generally the preferable choice.

Problems with imported data

Importing data can pose numerous challenges, particularly when dealing with messy datasets. This issue frequently arises when data has been manually entered by humans, such as in surveys featuring open-ended responses.

When respondents have the freedom to input data as they see fit, inconsistencies like variations in capitalization and spelling (e.g., "Dog" vs. "dog" vs. "dogs") can abound.

Similar to renovating a cluttered house, cleaning and organizing your data are essential steps to render it functional. This process remains critical even when dealing with initially disorganized data, as you must make do with what you have. Data wrangling entails transforming raw data into a format suitable for analysis. The extent of wrangling required varies depending on the circumstances. While medical and government data collection systems tend to be well-structured, other fields, particularly those involving survey data with free-text responses, often demand substantial cleaning and organization before analysis can commence.

Another challenge in dealing with data arises when it becomes incomprehensible to the analyst, which differs from simply being messy. Incomprehensible data may be impeccably organized but within a subject area unfamiliar to the analyst. For instance, deciphering medical coding, such as ICD-9 codes, can prove daunting without prior familiarity. There's no shame in seeking guidance from experts to gain a clearer understanding of the data.

As an analyst, it's often necessary to collaborate with domain experts. For instance, in a project involving neurological assessments for stroke victims, meeting with the overseeing physician might be essential to interpret the data on swallowing assessments.

Additionally, it's crucial to consider potential biases inherent in your data. Even seemingly straightforward sales data can be biased. For example, your dataset might only capture certain types of transactions or specific customer segments, impacting the validity of your analysis. It's essential to remain vigilant of these biases and assess their influence on your findings. For instance, sales data from Black Friday or the week preceding Christmas might not reflect typical buying patterns but rather emphasize particular high-traffic periods. Similarly, data from a store located in an affluent area might not accurately represent general purchasing behavior but rather the buying habits of more affluent clientele. These biases can compromise the reliability of your analysis, especially if the data isn't randomly sampled. This issue is significant and often overlooked.

Structured vs unstructured data

Next, let's distinguish between structured and unstructured data.

Comparing Structured and Unstructured Data

Category	Structured Data	Unstructured Data
Format	Organized, tabular	Free-form, no fixed structure
Examples	Spreadsheets, SQL DBs	Emails, images, videos
Storage	Relational databases	Data lakes, NoSQL, cloud storage
Processing	Easy analysis (SQL)	Requires AI, NLP, data mining

Structured data

This is the traditional row-and-column spreadsheet data that most analyses are based on. It's organized, easy to manipulate, and supports straightforward querying using languages like SQL (Structured Query Language).

Unstructured data

This includes text, images, and videos—types of data not organized in a predefined manner. You can't analyze unstructured data directly; it requires significant preprocessing to convert it into a structured format. For instance, with text data, you might need to create a table of word frequencies, removing punctuation and common words like "and" or "or." This book will not be diving into unstructured data much because we're not quite there yet. Unstructured data needs to be organized into a structured format to be usable. This is a topic deserving of much additional coverage.

While structured data is stored in databases using SQL, unstructured data can be stored in data warehouses, although analyzing it is much more complex. Proper preprocessing is crucial to convert unstructured data into a format suitable for analysis. In summary, while structured data is straightforward and widely used, unstructured data offers vast potential but requires careful preprocessing.

Review Questions

1. How can you get data?
2. Why are CSV files a good choice?
3. What can make data messy?
4. What's the difference between structured and unstructured data?
5. Can data be biased? Give an example.

2-2 Data dictionary

Learning Outcomes

2-2-1 Explain what a data dictionary is and why it's helpful.

2-2-2 Identify the parts of a data dictionary, like variable names, types, and labels.

2-2-3 Understand what coded values and summary statistics are.

2-2-4 Know that exploring new data often means checking the dictionary and running your own summaries.

Ideally, you'll have access to a data dictionary, which provides detailed information about the data, including definitions, types, and formats. A good data dictionary enhances the understanding and usability of the data, streamlining the analytical process. Understanding your data involves not just knowing the data itself but also understanding the types of data, variable names, and all associated details. This information is known as metadata. Unfortunately, data dictionaries are not always available.

Here's an example of a data dictionary from the IPEDS (Integrated Postsecondary Education Data System) dataset (US government department of education pubic information data), covering data from 1987 to 2012. This is government data, presented in an Excel format, which includes lists of different variables with comprehensive definitions.

#	Variable	Type	Label	Calculated	Source	Definition- From IPEDS glossary and Data Dictionary unless variable is calculated.	New/Revised Variable
1	groupid	Num	Group ID	No		This variable is used in the creation of matched sets, determined by the flags variable. If the GroupID is negative it represents a single institution; if the GroupID is positive it represents a group of institutions.	
2	academicyear	Num	Academic Year	No		The period of time generally extending from September to June, usually equated to 2 semesters or trimesters, 3 quarters, or the period covered by a 4-1-4 calendar system. Academic year is displayed as the end year (i.e. academic year 2010 includes data for 2009-2010).	
3	unitid_linchpin	Num	Unit ID Linchpin	No		The unit id is the primary (parent) id for a group of institutions or the unit id of the individual institution.	
4	unitid	Num	Unit ID	No	Institutional Characteristics	Unique identification number assigned to postsecondary institutions surveyed through the Integrated Postsecondary Education Data System (IPEDS). Also referred to as UNITID or IPEDS ID.	
5	isgrouped	Num	Institution is grouped	Yes		Institutions are grouped together based on how they report financial data. If an institution has a 'parent' institution and does not report their own financial data they are grouped with the parent institution.	
6	instname	Char	Institution Name	No	Institutional Characteristics	Name of the institution.	
7	TCSName	Char	Institution/Group name in TCS Online	No		Name of the institution as it appears in TCS Online, in some cases clarifying information has been added to the standard IPEDS institution names, such as state for institutions with the same name, or system name for grouped institutions. Only institutions that appear in TCS Online will have a TCSname (public and private nonprofit research, master's, bachelor's, and public community colleges within the U.S.).	
8	city	Char	City	No	Institutional Characteristics	City where the institution is located.	

In the data dictionary, you will find:

- Variable Name- A concise identifier for the variable.

- Variable Type- Specifies the type of data (e.g., integer, string).

- Label-A more descriptive name for the variable, which can be longer and more informative than the variable name.

- Calculated -Indicates whether the data is source data or derived.

- Source Information- Details where the data originates, such as the Census or other government entities.

- Description-A detailed explanation of what the variable represents.

This comprehensive dictionary (in Excel) also has sheets on:

- Coded Values: For instance, the number 1 might represent a specific state like Alabama or Alaska. These coded values are crucial for understanding categorical data. For example, the variable names and coded values might look like this:

Variable Name: STATE

Coded Value: 1 = Alabama, 2 = Alaska, etc.

	Clipboard				Font			

A1   ⌄   :   ✕ ✓ *fx*   value isgrouped

	A	B	C	D
1	value isgrouped			
2	0='Not grouped'			
3	1='Grouped' ;			
4				
5	value ansi_code			
6	1='Alabama'			
7	2='Alaska'			
8	4='Arizona'			
9	5='Arkansas'			
10	6='California'			
11	8='Colorado'			
12	9='Connecticut'			
13	10='Delaware'			
14	11='District of Columbia'			
15	12='Florida'			
16	13='Georgia'			
17	15='Hawaii'			
18	16='Idaho'			
19	17='Illinois'			

- Frequencies and Percentages: Frequency tables show how often each value occurs within the dataset, along with the percentage of occurrences.

A1   ∨ ⋮   *fx*   Variable name

	A	B	C	D	E	F	G	H	I
1	Variable name	Variable label	Code value	Value label	Frequency	Percent			
2	isgrouped	institution is grouped	0	Not grouped	199529	92.54			
3	isgrouped	institution is grouped	1	Grouped	16084	7.46			
4	ansi_code	ANSI code	1	Alabama	2981	1.38			
5	ansi_code	ANSI code	2	Alaska	792	0.37			
6	ansi_code	ANSI code	4	Arizona	3542	1.64			
7	ansi_code	ANSI code	5	Arkansas	2790	1.29			
8	ansi_code	ANSI code	6	California	25284	11.73			
9	ansi_code	ANSI code	8	Colorado	3917	1.82			
10	ansi_code	ANSI code	9	Connecticut	3133	1.45			
11	ansi_code	ANSI code	10	Delaware	559	0.26			
12	ansi_code	ANSI code	11	District of Columbia	891	0.41			
13	ansi_code	ANSI code	12	Florida	9654	4.48			
14	ansi_code	ANSI code	13	Georgia	4964	2.3			
15	ansi_code	ANSI code	15	Hawaii	939	0.44			
16	ansi_code	ANSI code	16	Idaho	921	0.43			
17	ansi_code	ANSI code	17	Illinois	9599	4.45			

- Summary Statistics: Basic statistics like mean values, which are essential for initial data exploration.

A1   ∨ ⋮   *fx*   Variable

	A	B	C	D	E	F	G	H
1	Variable	Label	N	Mean	Std Dev	Minimum	Maximum	
2	cpi_index	CPI Index	215613	162	34	111	228	
3	cpi_scalar_2012	CPI scalar	215613	1	0	0	1	
4	hepi_index	HEPI Index	215613	192	52	121	293	
5	hepi_scalar_2012	HEPI scalar	215613	1	0	0	1	
6	heca_index	HECA Index	215613	69	16	46	100	
7	heca_scalar_2012	HECA scalar	215613	1	0	0	1	
8	fte_count	Total fall FTE student enrollment	151599	2110	5767	0	380232	
9	fte12mn	Total 12-month FTE student enrollme	53293	2801	8664	0	768135	
10	tuition01	Unrestricted tuition and fees revenu	34848	13413691	31238661	110	599601984	
11	tuition02	Restricted tuition and fees revenue	6072	1009542	11266341	1	408876000	
12	tuition03	Gross tuition and fees revenue	116067	20066474	61927941	-1032198	3552223903	
13	nettuition01	Net tuition and fees revenue	115237	16490966	51325015	-2736278713	3269543856	

Additionally, the data dictionary includes some SAS-specific information since IPEDS uses SAS for data analysis.

Understanding the contents of your data and using a data dictionary is essential. As shown in the example, a data dictionary provides detailed information about each variable, including names, types, labels, and descriptions. It serves as a vital reference for anyone working with the data, ensuring clarity and consistency in its usage.

While a data dictionary is highly beneficial, it often includes only the basics needed for initial data exploration and understanding. When working with new data, you'll typically have to explore the data and calculate summary statistics to understand your variables better. This preparatory phase might take a bit of time and is essential work. It involves familiarizing yourself with terms and variables, such as understanding what "operations and plant maintenance" or "total expenditures on interest" mean in each context.

Review Questions

1. What is a data dictionary?
2. Name two things you might find in a data dictionary.
3. What are coded values? Give an example.
4. Why are summary statistics useful when working with new data?
5. What should you do if a data dictionary is missing or unclear?

2-3 Exploring data

Learning Outcomes

2-3-1 Understand what exploratory data analysis (EDA) is and why it's useful.

2-3-2 Use frequency tables to check for errors in data.

2-3-3 Summarize numbers using stats like mean, median, and range.

2-3-4 Use simple graphs (histograms, box plots, scatter plots) to spot patterns and problems.

2-3-5 Find outliers using graphs or stats (like IQR or z-scores).

2-3-6 Understand how z-scores help compare different data.

2-3-7 Spot missing data and think about why it's missing.

Moving on to explanatory analysis, where you delve further into the data looking at the variables you will be working with to understand their characteristics. Exploratory data analysis uses basic statistics techniques typically

taught in an introductory statistics course. Graphs and charts can complement summary statistics, providing visual representations of the data's characteristics and aiding in interpretation. When you embark on this journey,
you're essentially acquainting yourself with your data. This initial step isn't
about delving into complex statistical analyses or mining techniques yet.
Instead, it's about conducting exploratory data analysis to gain familiarity
with your dataset before diving into mining and to find issues with the data.

Frequency tables and distributions

Frequency tables and distributions are versatile tools applicable to all types
of data, making them indispensable for any data analysis task. They're
straightforward to generate, often available in basic statistical software, and
provide a solid foundation for understanding and exploring your dataset.

Frequency tables allow you to assess the cleanliness of your data and identify any unusual outliers. Frequency tables offer a concise summary of data
occurrences, making it easy to spot irregularities like spelling errors or duplicate entries, which can provide valuable insights for data cleaning. Histograms, which visualize data distributions, provide a clear visual representation, especially for quantitative variables. Anomalies, if present, become
evident, aiding in the identification of potential issues.

	Row Labels ▼	Count of Gender
2		
3	**Row Labels** ▼	**Count of Gender**
4	F	1
5	Female	5
6	M	2
7	Male	4
8	(blank)	
9	**Grand Total**	**12**
10		

Summary statistics

When it comes to basic summary statistics, they are primarily applicable to quantitative data and these stats offer valuable insights into the data's characteristics. Quantitative variables should be explored with basic summary statistics. Most software has easy functionality to do basic metrics of center (median, mean, mode) and spread (range, standard deviation) as well as the 5 number summary on numeric variables (min, Q1, median, Q3, max).

Mean	40.28
Median	39.50
Mode	41.00
Standard Deviation	11.64
Range	46.00

Visual exploration

Visualizing data is another indispensable aspect, although it comes with its challenges. Beyond two variables, interpreting visualizations becomes more complex, often requiring intricate techniques like lattice plots or drilldowns. However, at this stage, the goal isn't to create elaborate visualizations for presentations or dashboards. Instead, it's about conducting exploratory visualizations to identify any quality issues or patterns within the data.

When it comes to visualization techniques like histograms and scatter plots, their effectiveness can be hindered by the sheer volume of data in large datasets. While data mining isn't exclusive to large datasets, it's important to note that visualization becomes less clear when dealing with substantial amounts of data. Instead of neatly illustrating patterns, the data may appear as a dense blob, making it challenging to discern meaningful insights.

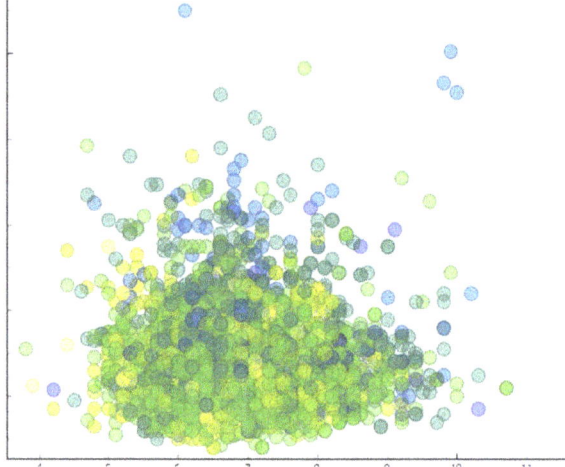

Outliers

Identifying outliers is a crucial aspect of data cleaning, often revealed through exploratory data analysis (EDA). Outliers, those data points that significantly deviate from the norm, can be visually detected, such as the points in the scatter plot that are notably distant from the rest.

Box plots offer another useful tool for outlier detection, providing a visual representation of data distribution and highlighting any extreme values beyond the whiskers.

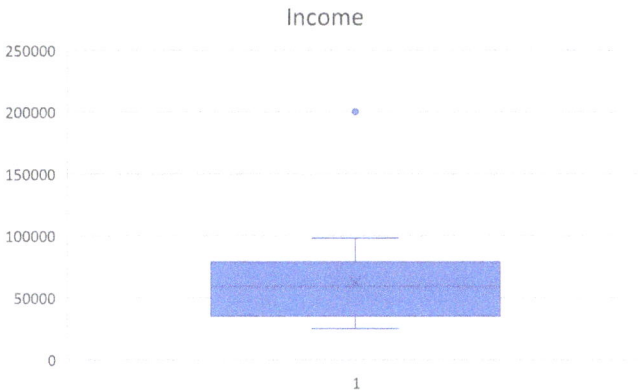

In statistics, the interquartile range (IQR) method is commonly used to identify outliers, where data points beyond 1.5 times the IQR from the first and third quartiles are flagged as outliers. While this method offers a quick and straightforward approach, outliers are often visually apparent, making them easier to identify with tools like box plots.

Normalizing data to detect outliers

Normalizing data involves transforming it to a standard scale, typically using z-scores from the standard normal distribution, which you may have encountered in your statistics studies. Let's review the basics here (with more to come as this topic becomes important in data mining). Imagine we have some random dataset, like test scores, for example. First, we calculate the mean (average) and the standard deviation, which measures the variability of the data. Then, we compute the z-score for each data point, which is obtained by subtracting the mean from the data point and dividing it by the standard deviation.

The resulting z-scores rescale the data, placing it on a standard normal distribution with a mean of 0 and a standard deviation of 1. Data points further away from the mean will have higher absolute z-scores, indicating their deviation from the average. For instance, a z-score of 2 signifies a data point that is two standard deviations above the mean.

Normalizing data to z-scores allows for comparability across different datasets with varying scales. Whether the original data is on a scale of 100 or 500, transforming it to z-scores ensures consistency in comparisons. This normalization process is particularly useful in data mining, as it removes the influence of measurement scales, making comparisons more robust and facilitating outlier identification.

By examining the z-scores, outliers can be identified based on their deviation from the mean. This approach complements other outlier detection techniques, such as the five-number summary method, providing a comprehensive means of identifying and addressing data anomalies.

In this method, outliers are flagged based on their z-scores. A z-score greater than or less than two standard deviations from the mean is typically considered an outlier. For instance, a data point with a z-score of 2.23, like the one corresponding to 105 in our example, would be regarded as extremely high.

Missing data

As for missing data, it's a common issue, though its impact varies depending on the context. Missing data is data that is not available or not recorded. In fields like medicine, where data recording is meticulous, missing data occurrences are less frequent. However, in cases where data is unavailable or goes unrecorded, missing data poses a challenge.

Interestingly, in data mining, missing data isn't always as prohibitive as it might seem. Since data mining is exploratory in nature, it's often less reliant on complete datasets compared to more structured statistical modeling. While missing data can still affect analyses, data mining techniques are often robust enough to accommodate some level of missingness without compromising results. Therefore, while missing data should be addressed where possible, its impact on data mining analyses may be less severe than in other analytical contexts.

Missing data is common in surveys and anywhere a human is given an option whether to fill in information, like when someone skips a question on a survey. It's not a huge deal since you can still analyze the other responses. But if data goes missing due to intentional deletion, that's a whole other issue. Deliberately removing data is unethical and can seriously mess up your analysis. When examining missing data be attentive to strange missing patterns such as one specific time frame missing or information about one person or location of a business. This is a flag that something is wrong with the data.

Detecting missing data is usually straightforward. You can often spot it through frequency distributions. For example, if you have 600 survey responses but only 583 entries for a particular question, you know you're missing some data. Some software, like SAS, even has built-in tools for analyzing missing data, but not all do. Still, you can usually figure it out on your own.

So, when you're working with data, always keep an eye out for missing data. It's just one of those things you'll likely encounter along the way.

Review Questions

1. What is the goal of exploratory data analysis?
2. How can a frequency table help clean your data?
3. Name two summary stats you can use for numeric data.
4. What kind of graph shows how data is spread out?
5. How do box plots help you spot outliers?
6. What does a z-score tell you about a data point?
7. What does it mean if a z-score is 2.5?
8. What are two common reasons data might be missing?
9. Why is it important to look for patterns in missing data?
10. How can you tell if data is missing in your dataset?

2-4 Role of the analyst

As the analyst, your role includes translating and making sense of the data, not just being a passive recipient of it. This might involve spending time on the phone, in Zoom meetings, or visiting the software creators to understand how the data was collected and what each field represents. For example, they might explain that a certain field represents the price tag scanned or the unit price. This communication is crucial for proper analysis.

Various systems generate data, and there might not always be someone who fully understands it at the point of data collection. Often, you might receive a large data dump, like the last six months of sales, with the expectation that you'll analyze it without much guidance. In such cases, you might need to contact the company that developed the software to get a clearer understanding of the data. The people you're working with might not understand the data themselves, which is why they hired you as an analyst.

Be prepared for this aspect of your job. Analysts don't just analyze data; they must first make sense of it. Before diving into data mining or other analytical tasks, you need a thorough understanding of your data.

Selecting the right variables to work with in analysis is crucial. You won't necessarily work with every single variable in your dataset. In many cases, you might have 100 variables but only a handful are relevant to your analysis. For example, you might only be interested in six key variables and not care about details like the store number where a sale occurred unless it's relevant to your analysis. You need to understand the data to select variables appropriately.

Chapter 3

Data Preprocessing

Data preprocessing is the essential step of preparing your data for mining. This involves data wrangling, which encompasses the tasks of cleaning, modifying, and restructuring data. Given the broad scope of data wrangling, this chapter will focus on key aspects and introduce important pre-processing techniques commonly used in data mining, such as principal component analysis.

2. Data
preprocessing

3-1 Data cleaning

Learning Outcomes

3-1-1 Define data cleaning and explain its purpose.

3-1-2 Identify and fix common data issues (e.g., type mismatches, out-of-range values).

3-1-3 Distinguish between missing and incomplete data.

3-1-4 Recognize and correct text, pattern, and field alignment errors.

3-1-5 Prepare a clean dataset suitable for analysis.

Data cleaning involves identifying and rectifying discrepancies in your dataset, such as inaccuracies and inconsistencies. Several common issues must be addressed before data analysis:

1. Data Type Inconsistency: This occurs when data entries do not conform to the expected format. For example, if respondents are asked to provide their ages as numbers but some enter their age as text, it creates inconsistencies by mixing numeric fields with character data.

2. Data Range Problems: These arise when entries fall outside the expected range. For instance, if a date is requested and someone enters the year as 2,300 instead of 2023, or if an age is entered as "2010" instead of "21." Such errors are common due to human input mistakes. Detecting these issues involves examining the minimum and maximum values and analyzing frequency distributions to identify outliers and anomalies.

3. Data Uniqueness: Ensuring that each entry is unique is critical, especially in datasets like sales records where duplicate entries might appear. Unique identifiers for each transaction help maintain data integrity, and key constraints in relational databases can enforce uniqueness.

4. Spelling and Capitalization Errors: Manual data entry often leads to in-

consistencies in spelling and capitalization. These errors can be rectified by standardizing text formats, such as converting all text to uppercase.

5. Set Membership: This ensures that categorical responses adhere to prede-fined options. For instance, responses for college year should be limited to freshman, sophomore, junior, or senior, avoiding entries like "second year."

6. Pattern Issues: Data formats like phone numbers or zip codes need to follow standard patterns. Inconsistencies can complicate analysis and must be standardized.

7. Cross-Field Issues: These involve verifying that multiple fields align logi-cally. For example, a person's age should correspond with their birthdate, or a product's price should match its category. Ensuring that data like "years in college" aligns with the respondent's academic status prevents inconsis-tencies.

8. Missing Data: Missing data can be problematic, particularly if it's sys-tematic. While some data mining algorithms can handle missing data, it is important to assess and address the extent of missing information.

9. Incomplete Data: Different from missing data, incomplete data refers to entries that are partially filled but lack critical information, such as an ad-dress missing the state.

10. Random Characters or Spaces: Text data can contain random characters or spaces that disrupt analysis. Cleaning these elements is necessary for accurate data processing.

Addressing these issues ensures that your dataset is accurate, consistent, and reliable, forming a solid foundation for subsequent data analysis.

Review Questions

1. What is data cleaning and why is it important?
2. Give an example of a type mismatch and how to fix it.
3. How can you identify values that are out of range?
4. Why is uniqueness important in data entries?
5. How do you fix spelling and capitalization issues?
6. What does set membership mean in data cleaning?
7. What is a pattern issue? Give an example.
8. Describe a cross-field error and how to detect it.
9. How is incomplete data different from missing data?
10. Why clean random characters or extra spaces?

3-2 Data modification

Learning Outcomes

3-2-1 Understand what data modification is and why it's useful after cleaning.

3-2-2 Rename columns to avoid confusion and improve clarity.

3-2-3 Reformat data values like zip codes or phone numbers.

3-2-4 Join or split data columns as needed (e.g., combine first and last names).

3-2-5 Group or bin data to make it easier to analyze or visualize.

Data modification, a secondary step after cleaning, involves altering clean data fields in some way to prepare them for analysis. After ensuring cleanliness, modifying data becomes essential for refining its representation, aiding in more effective analysis. Let's delve into data modification scenarios.

When preparing to merge datasets, if both contain a column labeled X but representing different variables, one must be renamed to avoid confusion.

Changing variable names is often crucial for clarity, especially if initial labels are unclear or redundant. Always preserve the original data and document modifications to maintain integrity.

In another instance, modifying data involves altering the structure of the data values. This might entail adjusting phone numbers to exclude area codes, assuming they're already standardized, because they need to be in a specific format. Reformatting zip codes is a typical example, simplifying data management by converting nine-digit codes to five digits for consistency and ease of analysis. This isn't cleaning; rather, it's optimizing data while ensuring uniformity.

Another common data modification task is joining or splitting fields. Joining fields combines separate data elements, like merging first and last names into a full name column. Conversely, splitting fields divides combined data into separate components, such as extracting first and last names from a single field.

Additionally, grouping and binning data are common data modifications, involves categorizing data into intervals or groups for better interpretation. Particularly with quantitative data, grouping is essential. This entails categorizing continuous variables into intervals for better analysis, enabling techniques like frequency distributions and graphical representations. Many software tools offer automated binning functionality, simplifying the process.

Grouping effectively converts quantitative data into categorical variables, facilitating analysis. For instance, salary data can be binned into categories like "greater than" or "less than or equal to" a certain threshold. Retaining the original data ensures flexibility and reproducibility in analysis.

Salary	<$60K
27000	Y
56000	Y
32000	Y
78000	N
98000	N
67000	N
40000	Y
...	

Grouped salary data.

Salary range
25000-34999
35000-44999
45000-54999
55000-64999
65000-74999
75000-84999
85000-94999
95000-104999
195000-204999

Another way to group salary data is by creating a binary variable, such as indicating whether a salary is above or below a certain threshold. Often creating ranges or groups is essential for generating histograms or charts, which can be easily done in Excel or other software. Custom categories can also be manually created if needed. This process is crucial for many data mining techniques and software tools.

Categorical data, although not continuous, may also benefit from grouping. For instance, pet data collected with various specific breeds could be grouped into broader categories like "cat" or "dog," or further refined into groups like "large dog" or "small dog" for simplicity and clarity.

Review Questions

1. Why do we need to change data after it's already clean?
2. How does renaming columns help when combining datasets?
3. What are the pros and cons of turning numbers into categories?
4. When should we split or join columns?
5. How does grouping data make analysis easier?

3-3 Data restructuring

Learning Outcomes

3-3-1 Understand what data restructuring means.

3-3-2 Change data formats (like from data frame to Tibble).

3-3-3 Switch between long and wide data formats.

3-3-4 Create summary tables with counts or averages.

3-3-5 Join datasets to add new information.

3-3-6 Make smaller datasets by picking certain rows or columns.

Beyond cleaning and modifying individual data points, restructuring the entire dataset is the next step. This involves operations on the entire data table, such as converting data types, summarizing data or subsetting the data.

A data table itself is a data type and can be changed (restructured). In R, for example, converting a regular data frame to a Tibble using the Tidy verse package is a common restructuring task. The Tibble has different properties from the original data frame. Similarly, in Excel, where data is typically organized into sheets, you can convert them into table formats, altering the data structure's properties.

Converting data from long to wide format and vice versa is a data restructuring common practice, especially when dealing with time columns. In the long format, years may be stacked vertically (e.g., 1990, 2000, 2010), whereas in the wide format, each year occupies its own column. This transformation is often necessary for analytics tools like SPSS, which require specific data formats for some types of analysis.

Aggregate data creation is another important aspect of data restructuring. This involves summarizing data into a pivot table-like format, aggregating information such as averages or counts. For example, instead of having individual student records, you might create an aggregated database showing the count of students in each class level (freshman, sophomore, etc.). This simplifies the database while retaining essential information for analysis and is often used for presentation and analytical graphs which need summarized data for interpretation. Typically, data mining will use non-aggregated data although one of the things data mining can do is find groups (clusters) in data which can be used for the aggregation structure.

Another aspect of data restructuring involves integrating data from other sources, a process commonly done through joins. For instance, you might join additional variables, such as population numbers for towns based on zip codes in your dataset. This is often necessary to enrich the existing data with supplementary information.

Creating a smaller or sub-set dataset is another restructuring approach, distinct from aggregation. Instead of using all available columns, you select only the relevant ones, forming a more focused analytical file. While this was once crucial due to computational limitations, modern technology makes it less necessary, though still beneficial for efficiency. For instance, you could subset data on people for individuals over 65 years old. This allows you to work with a refined dataset tailored to your analysis needs.

Review Questions

1. What is data restructuring?
2. What's the difference between a data frame and a Tibble in R?
3. When would you use long vs. wide format?
4. Why would you create a summary (like a count or average)?
5. What does a data join do?
6. Why make a smaller dataset?

3-4 Normalizing data

Learning Outcomes

3-4-1 Understand what normalization means.

3-4-2 Explain what a z-score is and how to calculate it.

3-4-3 Know why z-scores help compare data on different scales.

3-4-4 Recognize when to use normalization in data analysis.

3-4-5 Know that z-scores only apply to quantitative data.

Normalization involves transforming data to adhere to a standard distribution, typically the standard normal distribution but there are other methods. In the standard normal distribution, the mean is zero and the standard deviation is one.

Area under
curve =1

−3   −2   −1   0   1   2   3

Z score

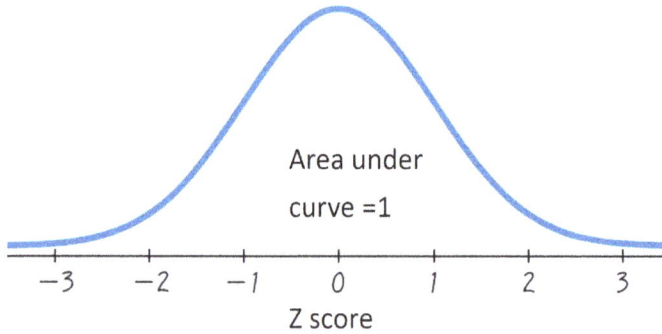

Crucially, this standardization creates "z-scores," which represent the number of standard deviations a data point is from the mean of that data. Converting data to z-scores makes it independent of measurement units, allowing for fair comparisons across different scales. For example, whether measuring height in inches or centimeters, converting to z-scores yields compa-
rable results. This scale-independent metric enhances the reliability and
interpretability of data mining analyses.

The formula for calculating z-scores is straightforward and can be easily implemented using software tools. By standardizing variables in this way, we
ensure consistency and robustness in our data analysis processes.

Converting Data to z scores

- Take quantitative data on a measurement scale, find the mean and standard deviation

$$z = \frac{x - \mu}{\sigma}$$

- Result is standardized (aka normalized) data all on the same scale of z scores

- Apply the formula to compute z

To compute a z-score, subtract the mean (denoted by μ, representing the population mean) from each data point and then divide by the standard deviation (denoted by σ). This yields a z-score, indicating how many standard deviations a data point is from the mean. A z-score of one signifies one standard deviation above the mean, while a z-score of zero corresponds to the mean itself.

Let's say we have a test score of 85. The average score (mean) of the class is 75, and the standard deviation is 10. Calculate the z sore:

$$z = \frac{x - \mu}{\sigma}$$

$$z = \frac{85 - 75}{10}$$

$$z = 1$$

So, the Z-score is 1. This means that the test score of 85 is 1 standard deviation above the mean.

Normalization, specifically calculating z-scores, is applicable only to quantitative data, not categorical data. Quantitative data can be either continuous or discrete, but regardless of its nature, z-score calculation follows a standardized formula.

Most software simplifies this process, with functionality for automatically calculating z-scores. However, it's essential to understand when to apply standardization. In data mining, where fair comparisons are vital for metrics such as distance, normalized data is preferred. Conversely, for descriptive statistics or summaries, retaining original units may be preferable.

In summary, normalizing data using z-scores is fundamental in data mining to mitigate the influence of measurement scales.

3-5 Reducing dimensionality

First off, let's touch on the Curse of Dimensionality. Essentially, when dealing with datasets with many variables, things get complicated. To put it simply, the more variables you have, the more complex your data becomes. While what constitutes "small" or "big" is subjective, having over 20 variables can start to make things feel hefty. And it's not uncommon to encounter datasets with many more variables than that.

The Curse of Dimensionality manifests as the volume of the data space exponentially increases with each additional variable. This leads to a sparse distribution of data points, making analysis, visualization, and modeling challenging.

Let's break it down further. In one dimension, like plotting age on a number line, it's straightforward. Move to two dimensions, and you're into XY coordinate territory, still manageable. But beyond three dimensions, things get tricky. Our brains are wired to comprehend and interact with three-dimensional space. Trying to visualize data in four or more dimensions becomes a mental gymnastics exercise. After all, our world is three-dimensional, and grasping concepts beyond that is tough.

So, what does the Curse of Dimensionality really mean? Essentially, when we're dealing with data in higher dimensions, our ability to analyze and model it accurately starts to falter. Our brains struggle to intuitively grasp and comprehend data in these higher-dimensional spaces. As a result, interpreting and explaining the results of models and analyses becomes challenging.

Enter dimension reduction, the antidote to this curse. The goal here is to decrease the number of dimensions in our dataset. But it's not as simple as just cherry-picking a couple of variables out of many. Instead, it involves creating new derived variables that capture the essence of the original ones, condensing the dataset into a more manageable size.

Let's visualize this concept. Imagine we have data plotted in a two-dimensional graph. By carefully selecting a single dimension, we can still capture much of the information present in the original two dimensions. This reduction from a higher to a lower dimension is at the heart of dimensionality reduction.

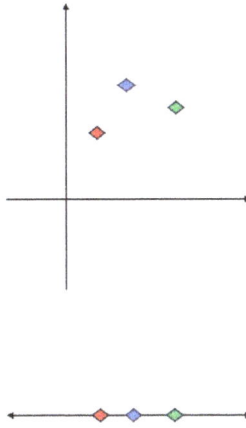

So, how do we actually reduce dimensions? The mathematical intricacies involve concepts like eigenvalues and decompositions, typically covered in higher mathematics courses like linear algebra. But a commonly used technique for dimension reduction is principal component analysis (PCA) which can be understood at a practical level without too much math.

Dimension reduction isn't merely about discarding variables; it's a more nuanced process. It's particularly prevalent in fields dealing with extensive datasets, such as bioinformatics. In these domains, datasets often exhibit high dimensionality, characterized by numerous variables rather than just many observations. So, it's not solely about the sample size (n), but also about the sheer volume of variables.

Review Questions

1. What is the Curse of Dimensionality?
2. Why is high-dimensional data hard to analyze or visualize?
3. What is dimensionality reduction?
4. Why not just delete some variables to reduce dimensions?
5. In what kinds of fields is dimensionality reduction especially useful?

3-6 Principal components analysis

Learning Outcomes

3-6-1 Explain the purpose of PCA and when to use it.

3-6-2 Interpret a scree plot to choose the number of components.

3-6-3 Understand how principal components summarize original variables.

Principal components analysis (PCA) is a key technique for reducing dimensionality. Through PCA, we transform the original n-dimensional data into a lower-dimensional space (K dimensions). This is achieved by creating new variables known as principal components. These components serve as amalgamations of the original variables, capturing their essence in a more condensed form.

Consider this illustration: imagine we have two-dimensional data represented by variables X and Y. The scatter plot of this data reveals points scattered across. Now, the line drawn through the plot isn't a regression line; rather, it represents a principal component. By combining the weights of the original variables, we create this principal component, effectively reducing the data from two dimensions to one along this component. Visually, it's akin to rotating the axes, condensing the information into a single dimension.

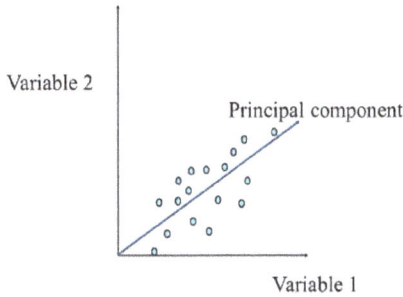

In essence, principal components serve as meta-variables, summarizing the underlying patterns of the original data in a more manageable form. Through PCA, we navigate the complexities of high-dimensional datasets, simplifying them for easier interpretation and analysis.

Now, let's dive into a real-world dataset: the cheese tasting dataset which collects data on acid levels and a taste rating on cheese. Here, we have 20 cases of cheese samples, each evaluated

Case	Acetic	H2S	Lactic	Taste
1	4.543	3.135	0.86	12.3
2	5.159	5.043	1.53	20.9
3	5.366	5.438	1.57	39
4	5.759	7.496	1.81	47.9
5	4.663	3.807	0.99	5.6
6	5.697	7.601	1.09	25.9
7	5.892	8.726	1.29	37.3
8	6.078	7.966	1.78	21.9
9	4.898	3.85	1.29	18.1
10	5.242	4.174	1.58	21
11	5.74	6.142	1.68	34.9
12	6.446	7.908	1.9	57.2
13	4.477	2.996	1.06	0.7
14	5.236	4.942	1.3	25.9
15	6.151	6.752	1.52	54.9
16	6.365	9.588	1.74	40.9
17	4.787	3.912	1.16	15.9
18	5.412	4.7	1.49	6.4
19	5.247	6.174	1.63	18
20	5.438	9.064	1.99	38.9
21	4.564	4.949	1.15	14

across four variables: acidity, sulfuric acid, lactic acid, and taste. While there are only four variables, we still need six plots to explore the two-by-two relationships adequately.

Bivariate relations in cheese data

Taste by H2S

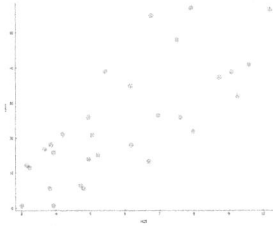

Taste by Lactic

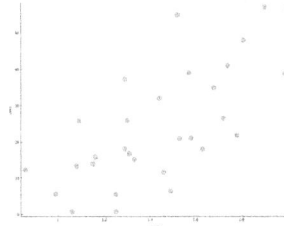

Bivariate relations in cheese data

Taste by Acetic

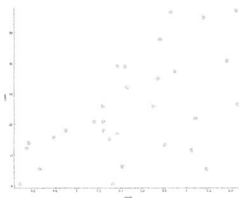

Lactic by H2S

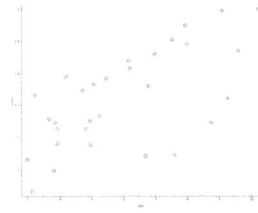

Bivariate relations in cheese data

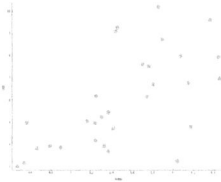

H2S by Acetic   **Lactic by Acetic**

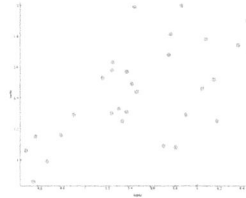

For example, when we examine the relationship between acetic acid and sulfuric acid, a linear pattern emerges. Each plot offers unique insights into the interaction between these variables, revealing their collective impact on the taste of the cheese. Across all the bivariate relationships, common linear patterns are evident. Although it's impossible to represent four-dimensional data on a single plot, analyzing the two-by-two relationships uncovers intriguing patterns. While the scatter plots do not show perfect correlations, discernible linear trends suggest potential redundancy among the variables.

Indeed, the variables seem to convey similar information about taste, indicating redundancy and collinearity. Given this redundancy, principal components analysis (PCA) emerges as a promising tool for dimension reduction. PCA aims to distill the essence of the original variables into a smaller set of meta-variables, or principal components, thus reducing dimensionality while preserving essential information. In our case, with four(N) original variables, we could derive one, two, three, or four (possible values of K) principal components as the number of principal components maximizes at the number of original variables (four in this case).

Scree plot

So, when it comes to determining the number of principal components (K) to retain, we aim for a balance between capturing information and reducing dimensionality. Technically, we could perform principal components analysis (PCA) up to the number of original variables, but with four informative variables, we typically aim for one, two, or three principal components. But how do we decide? The key lies in examining a scree plot, a graphical representation of the proportion of variability captured by each principal component. In simpler terms, it shows how much information each component holds.

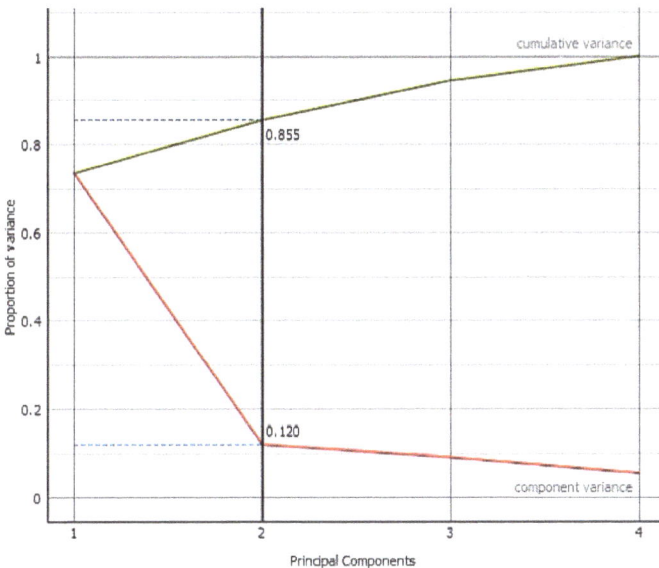

Here's how it works: The orange curve in the scree plot represents the proportion of variability captured by each principal component. For instance, if the first principal component captures 70% of the variability, that's quite substantial. However, we don't stop there. We examine where the curve "elbows," indicating diminishing returns in terms of information captured.

In our example, the curve starts to level off after the first two components, with the third component adding only a marginal increase in variability capture. So, by retaining the first two principal components, which collectively capture around 85% of the variability, we strike a balance between reducing dimensionality and retaining essential information.

Technically, you could extend the analysis to three principal components, but remember our goal is to reduce dimensionality. Going from four original variables to three principal components doesn't offer significant reduction. And if we retain all four principal components, we're essentially keeping the same number of components as variables, which defeats the purpose of dimensionality reduction. So, two principal components seem to be the optimum choice.

Principal component variables

Principal components are new variables derived from linear combinations of the original variables. In the case of the cheese data, we'll generate two new variables, PC1 and PC2, which will capture the essence of the original variables.

Computing the actual values of the principal component variables is rather complex. Fortunately, software tools can handle the calculations for us, saving us from the manual labor of performing complex linear algebra. So now, we'll obtain two new derived variables that capture the essence of the original four variables.

Looking at the table, the first columns represent the original data, while the last two columns are our new variables, PC1 and PC2. Each row corresponds to a cheese sample, with its associated values for the original variables and the newly derived principal components.

	PC1 0.735363	PC2 0.119653	Acetic	H2S	Lactic	Taste
variance						
1	-2.86007	-0.627133	4.543	3.135	0.86	12.3
2	-0.470934	-0.34678	5.159	5.043	1.53	20.9
3	0.448528	-0.622224	5.366	5.438	1.57	39
4	1.97352	-0.566906	5.759	7.496	1.81	47.9
5	-2.59117	-0.352425	4.663	3.807	0.99	5.6
6	0.024672	0.211696	5.697	7.601	1.09	25.9
7	1.16833	-0.0042988	5.892	8.726	1.29	37.3
8	1.46652	0.653796	6.078	7.966	1.78	21.9
9	-1.47677	-0.467286	4.898	3.85	1.29	18.1
10	-0.528564	-0.155509	5.242	4.174	1.58	21
11	0.986182	-0.0365258	5.74	6.142	1.68	34.9
12	3.0968	0.129492	6.446	7.908	1.9	57.2
13	-2.98511	-0.432245	4.477	2.996	1.06	0.7
14	-0.659011	-0.295926	5.236	4.942	1.3	25.9
15	1.85171	-0.0165728	6.151	6.752	1.52	54.9
16	2.64876	0.379249	6.365	9.588	1.74	40.9
17	-1.84386	-0.534885	4.787	3.912	1.16	15.9
18	-0.879706	0.513921	5.412	4.7	1.49	6.4
19	-0.043783	-0.268583	5.247	6.174	1.63	18
20	2.10734	-0.995135	5.438	9.064	1.99	38.9
21	-1.85154	-0.913861	4.564	4.949	1.15	14
22	-0.832893	0.0797647	5.298	5.22	1.33	15.2
23	1.01509	-0.606847	5.455	9.242	1.44	32
24	3.32357	-1.00585	5.855	10.199	2	56.71
25	-1.1421	0.292548	5.366	3.664	1.31	16.8
26	-0.603898	1.46905	6.043	3.219	1.46	11.6
27	1.58151	1.20951	6.458	6.962	1.72	26.5
28	-1.73213	0.7087	5.328	3.912	1.25	0.7
29	-0.533182	0.834613	5.802	6.685	1.08	13.4
30	-0.657818	1.76665	6.176	4.787	1.25	5.5

It is important to note that the principal components were computed from normalized data (vs original data on measurement scale – note the table shows original measurement scale). It's essential to note that using non-normalized values would yield completely different results. If original scale variables are used values with larger scales would distort the results.

This ensures consistency and accuracy in the dimension reduction process (the principal components remain the same if the measurement scale is changed since they are based on normalized data). These new variables, PC1 and PC2, are crucial. With them, we can effectively discard the original four variables and still work with meaningful data. For instance, we can perform cluster analysis directly on these principal components. This approach simplifies visualization and analysis, especially when dealing with high-dimensional data.

Weights

So, where do these values of the principal component variables come from?

Coefficients, often referred to as weights, play a crucial role in understanding principal components.

These weights are extracted from the software, usually presented in a table format. Think of them like the coefficients in the equation of a line, but with a twist. From the software, you'll obtain these coefficients, which essentially tell you how much each original variable contributes to the principal component.

Feature name	PC1 0.735363	PC2 0.119653
Acetic	0.466074	0.8509
H2S	0.515302	-0.202832
Lactic	0.502443	-0.0945225
Taste	0.514578	-0.475284

For example, let's take Principal Component 1 (PC1). We have four original variables: acetic acid, sulfuric acid, lactic acid, and taste. Each of these variables is associated with a weight, indicating its influence on PC1. So, if we have weights of 0.46, 0.51, 0.50, and 0.51 respectively for these variables, the calculation for PC1 becomes:

PC1=0.46*acetic +0.51*h2s + 0.50*lactic + 0.51*taste

By plugging in the respective weights and values of the normalized data, you could calculate values of PC1 and PC2 using very simple algebra.

Interpretation of principal components

Now, instead of thinking about the cheese data in terms of the original four variables, we can consider it in terms of the two principal component variables. Although we sacrificed a bit of information, capturing 85% of the data information, we simplified our analysis by working with fewer variables. This simplification is crucial, especially when dealing with large datasets with numerous variables.

Throughout this course, we primarily use original data. However, keep in mind that many analyses can also be conducted on principal components. Since principal components encapsulate the essence of the variables, they are incredibly useful for various analyses like clustering. Thus, understanding and utilizing principal components effectively can significantly enhance data analysis processes.

Interpreting the weights assigned to each variable may require some domain expertise. In the case of the cheese data, the weights seem relatively straightforward. For example, the first principal component evenly weighs all cheese tasting information, while the second heavily emphasizes acetic acid, contrasting with taste. While this interpretation might not always be straightforward, understanding the patterns in the weights can provide valuable insights.

Don't hesitate to consult with experts familiar with the data when analyzing principal components. While they may lack analytical skills, their knowledge of the data's context can help interpret the results effectively. Ultimately, leveraging principal components can enhance data analysis processes, providing deeper insights into complex datasets.

So, the gist of principal components is this: they're a handy tool for dealing with large datasets. Imagine you're faced with a dataset containing hundreds of variables. It's just not feasible to work with all of them directly. That's where principal components come in. They allow you to distill the essence of your data into a more manageable number of derived variables. In practical terms, this means taking those 100 variables and condensing them down to, say, seven or six derived variables. This reduction in dimensionality makes it much easier to analyze the data effectively.

With modern software, the process is quite straightforward to use principal components. You don't need to crunch numbers manually like in the old days. The software does the heavy lifting for you. They're a valuable tool for making sense of big datasets and extracting meaningful insights. And the best part? They're not as hard to use as you might think. So, next time you're faced with a mountain of data, remember the power of principal components. They just might be your new best friend in data analysis.

Review Questions

1. What problem does PCA help solve in data analysis?
2. Why do we normalize data before applying PCA?
3. What does a scree plot help you decide?
4. How many principal components can you have in a dataset with four variables?
5. What do the weights in a principal component tell you?
6. How can PCA help with data visualization?

Chapter 4

Cluster Analysis

In this chapter, we will begin exploring the techniques of data mining, starting with cluster analysis. Cluster analysis is a technique used to group a set of objects in such a way that objects in the same group (or cluster) are more like each other than to those in other groups.

4-1 Unsupervised learning

Cluster analysis falls under a category of algorithms known as unsupervised learning. This concept originates from machine learning, a field where algorithms learn patterns from data without predefined labels.

Learning Outcomes

4-1-1 Tell the difference between labeled and unlabeled data.

4-1-2 Explain what unsupervised learning is and how it differs from supervised learning.

4-1-3 Understand what clustering is and why it's useful.

4-1-4 Know when and why to use clustering with data that has no labels.

4-1-5 Recognize that clustering helps find patterns in new or unknown data.

Labeled vs. unlabeled data

When dealing with a dataset, it may or may not include labels. Labels can be thought of as tags or identifiers. Typically, a label is a categorical variable with a finite set of values, such as "yes" or "no." For instance, if we consider whether an object is a tree, the label could be "yes" or "no."

Consider items in a grocery store. Each item can be labeled with a category, like "vegetable," "fruit," or "herb." If we have this category column, our data is labeled. However, if we lack this category column, we have unlabeled data.

Labeled data has a categorical variable serving as a tag or identifier. With labeled data, we perform tasks such as prediction and classification. These methods are referred to as supervised learning because the labels "supervise" the learning process by providing a reference for what each data point represents. For example, knowing that cilantro is an herb and tomato is a vegetable allows us to train a model based on these categories.

Food	Labelled Category
Cilantro	Herb
Tomato	Vegetable
Butternut squash	Vegetable
Zucchini	Vegetable
Orange	Fruit

Unlabeled data does not contain predefined labels. An example of unlabeled data might include a set of eight binary variables with no clear identification or grouping information. Without labels, it's challenging to group or organize this data effectively.

	A	B	C	D	E	F	G	H	I	J
1	id	Var1	Var2	Var3	Var4	Var5	Var6	Var7	Var8	
2	1	1	0	1	0	0	1	0	1	
3	2	1	0	0	0	1	0	0	1	
4	3	0	0	0	0	0	0	0	0	
5	4	0	0	0	0	0	0	0	0	
6	5	0	1	0	0	0	0	0	0	
7	6	1	0	0	1	0	0	0	1	
8	7	1	0	1	1	1	0	0	1	
9	8	0	0	0	1	0	0	0	0	
10	9	0	0	0	0	0	0	0	0	
11	10	0	1	1	0	0	0	0	0	
12	11	1	0	0	0	1	0	0	1	
13	12	0	1	0	0	0	0	0	0	
14	13	0	1	0	0	0	0	0	0	

This chapter will focus on techniques for analyzing unlabeled data, known as unsupervised learning in machine learning parlance. In unsupervised learning, we explore the structure and patterns within the data without pre-defined categories.

Purpose of clustering

When you have novel data without predefined labels, it's challenging to group or organize this data effectively. Clustering techniques can help here. These techniques are examples of unsupervised algorithms; a concept rooted in machine learning and AI. With no categorical variable to classify the data values, the goal is to discover the underlying structure of the data.

Working with unlabeled data is often a precursor to eventually labeling it. It's a crucial first step, which is why we address it at the beginning of our exploration. Unsupervised algorithms help in finding patterns within the data, making it an exploratory technique. Data mining aims to uncover these patterns and relationships before applying other data analysis methods.

In unsupervised data mining, there are two primary techniques: clustering and association. This chapter, we'll focus on clustering, and in a subsequent week, we'll cover association, a different type of unsupervised data mining.

Review Questions

1. What is labeled data? What is unlabeled data?
2. Why is clustering called "unsupervised" learning?
3. How is supervised learning different from unsupervised learning?
4. In a grocery store, what would be an example of labeled data?

4-2 Clustering and distance

Learning Outcomes

4-2-1 Define clustering and its purpose.

4-2-2 Compute Euclidean distance in 2D, 3D, and higher dimensions.

4-2-3 Use distance to measure similarity between data points.

4-2-4 Compare distance metrics: Euclidean, Jaccard, Mahalanobis, Minkowski.

4-2-5 Create and interpret a distance matrix.

4-2-6 Explain the need for data normalization in clustering.

4-2-7 Apply distance calculations manually or with tools.

Clustering involves grouping data points based on their similarities. This technique uses mathematical distance to measure similarity, helping to uncover the structure of the data by comparing how far apart different values are.

To understand clustering, we first need to learn how to calculate mathematical distance. This concept should be familiar from geometry and math. For instance, the Pythagorean theorem leads to the distance formula, which calculates the distance between two points.

Mathematical distance is a key concept in clustering. It refers to how far apart two points are in space. For example, if you've used a ruler to measure the length of an object, you've measured distance. In geometry, the distance between two points is the shortest line connecting them.

Basics of computing distance

In everyday physical space distance is the shortest measurement between two locations. This is the straightforward measurement between two points, such as the shortest line between a block and an oval.

In algebra, you might have encountered problems where you needed to calculate the distance between two points on a coordinate plane. In the Cartesian (x and y) plane two points can be plotted and connected with a segment. The length of the segment is distance between which is easy to measure when the segment is vertical or horizontal. For example, the distance between points (1, 1) and (1, 4) is 3, as they share the same x-value and differ by 3 units on the y-axis.

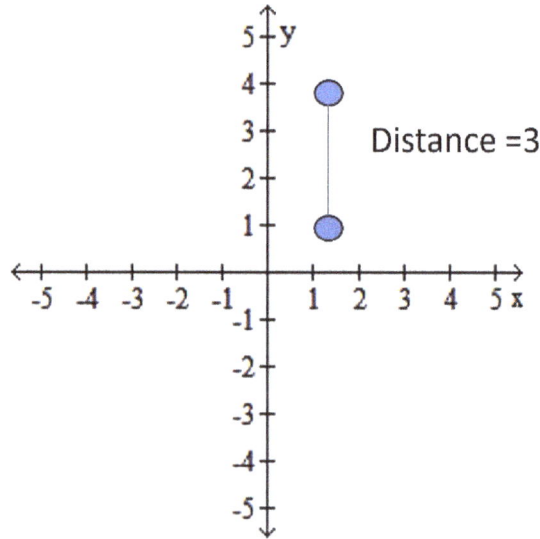

When dealing with points in a two-dimensional space that cannot easily be connected by a vertical or horizontal segment, the distance formula (derived from the Pythagorean theorem) helps calculate how far apart the points are.

Euclidean distance is the application of the Pythagorean theorem in a coordinate system.

The concept of mathematical distance is rooted in the Pythagorean theorem. According to the theorem, in a right triangle with sides a and b, the length of the hypotenuse c is given by:

$$c = \sqrt{a^2 + b^2}$$

When we refer to Euclidean distance in data analysis, we're measuring how far apart points are in a multidimensional space.

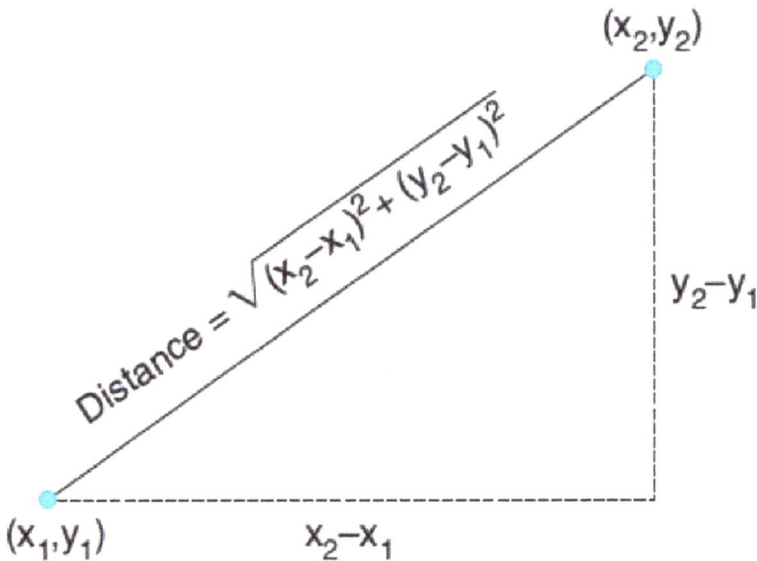

The distance formula derived from the Pythagorean theorem substitutes for the sides the vertical and horizontal lengths of the right triangle as computed on the coordinate plane with the horizontal side length being the difference of the x coordinates and the vertical side length the difference of the y coordinates.

For example, consider two points (1, 4) and (-4, 1) on a Cartesian plane. Plugging these values into the distance formula:

Distance= = 7.07

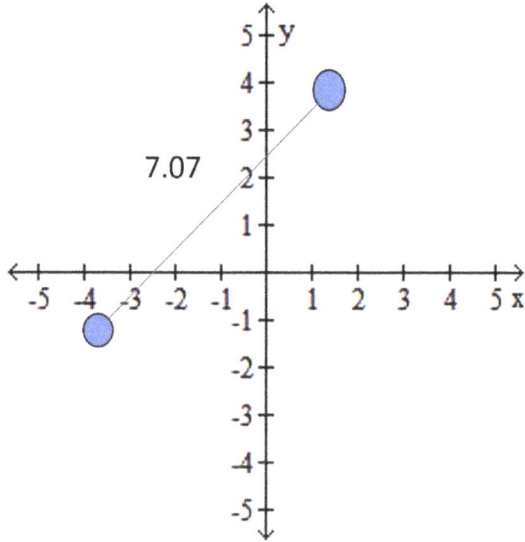

This formula extends to higher dimensions, allowing us to measure distances in three-dimensional space and beyond. The 2-d Cartesian plane extends to a 3-d plane easily and points can be located with x, y, and z coordinates.

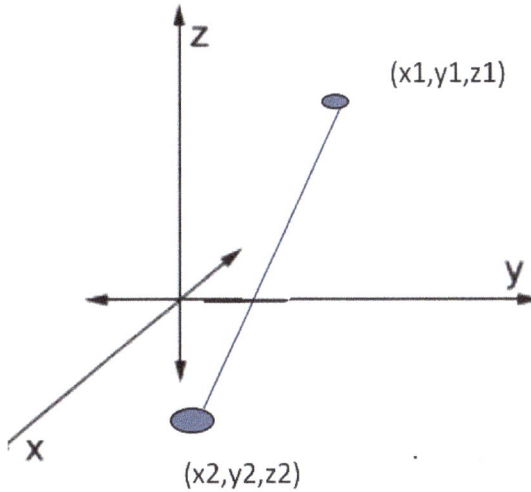

For three-dimensional space, The Euclidean distance formula extends to compute distance between two points in three-dimensional space to include the z-axis:

$$distance = \sqrt{(z_2 - z_1)^2 + (y_2 - y_1)^2 + (x_2 - x_1)^2}$$

Using the basic distance formula, calculating the distance between two points in two-dimensional or three-dimensional space is straightforward. However, we can extend this concept to any number of dimensions. This is crucial in data analysis because data often exists in multidimensional space, with each dimension representing a variable. Abstractly instead of using x,y,z we can label the first point P with coordinates p1, p2 and p3 for 3-d space and the second point Q with coordinates q1, q2 and q3 for 3-d space.

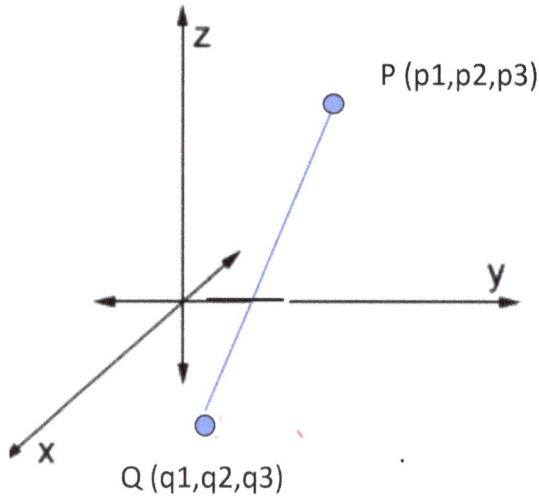

The distance formula can be written as:

$$distance = \sqrt{(p_3 - q_3)^2 + (p_2 - q_2)^2 + (p_1 - q_1)^2}$$

While humans can't visualize beyond three dimensions, in data analysis, we routinely work with datasets that have many variables. The number of dimensions in data space corresponds to the number of variables in a dataset. Despite the challenge of visualizing higher dimensions, we can still calculate distances in these spaces using a generalized formula.

Generalizing distance

In a multidimensional space, we can generalize the distance formula. If we have points P and Q in n-dimensional space the Euclidean distance between them is:

$$distance = \sqrt{\sum_{k=1}^{n}(p_k - q_k)^2}$$

This formula allows us to calculate the distance between any two points regardless of the number of variables (dimensions) they have. This generalization is known as Euclidean distance, and it's the most used distance metric in data analysis.

Other distance metrics

While Euclidean distance is widely used, there are other distance metrics suitable for different scenarios. Euclidean distance is used on continuous measurable variables and can be used for discrete variables as well. However, other data types and situations may be more suited to other distance metrics.

Binary data consists of values like 0 and 1, often representing yes/no or true/false responses. Binary data is common in many datasets, such as survey responses where people answer yes or no to various questions. For binary data, the Jaccard distance is a more appropriate metric than Euclidean distance. The Jaccard distance measures dissimilarity between sets of binary values.

When variables are correlated the Mahalanobis distance may be used. This metric accounts for covariance between variables. Another metric frequently used is the Minkowski distance metric which is a generalization of the Euclidean distance metric. These metrics are implemented in data analysis software, so you don't need to calculate them manually. The software will choose the appropriate metric based on your data and analysis requirements.

Applying distance to clustering

In clustering, the goal is to group similar data points together. By calculating the distances between data points, we can determine which points are closer to each other and should be grouped into the same cluster. This process is fundamental to many data mining and machine learning tasks, enabling us to discover patterns and structures within large datasets. To summarize, clustering is an unsupervised data mining method that relies on distance metrics to group data based on similarity.

Clustering algorithms use these various distance metrics depending on the type of data. Euclidean distance is the most common metric used for clustering, but other metrics like Mahalanobis or Jaccard distances might be applied depending on the nature of the data. Normalized data is generally used for clustering.

Let's look at a simple dataset with four observations and two variables, X and Y. Here are the observations:

	x	y
A	1	2
B	2	2
C	3	8
D	4	9

These points are plotted on a Cartesian plane like an algebra class and can be visualized.

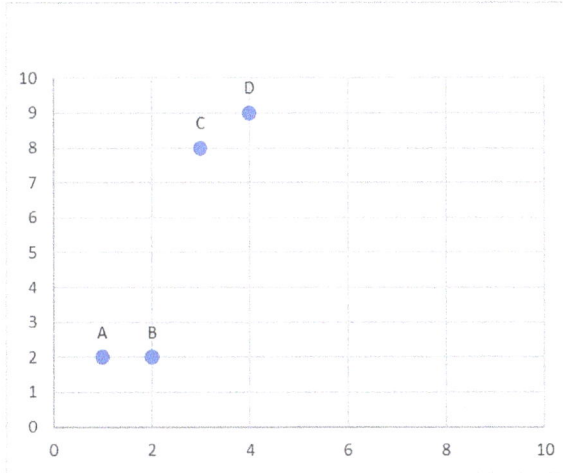

Using the distance formula distances between the points can be computed. These calculations can be done by hand, using Excel, or by employing data analysis software. Calculated distances for all pairs of points are:

Point to Point	Distance
A to B	1
B to C	6.082763
C to D	1.414214
D to A	7.615773
A to C	6.324555
B to D	7.28011

Understanding and calculating distances between data points are foundational steps in clustering. By knowing the distances, we can determine which points are close to each other and should be grouped together.

Distance matrix

A better way to visualize distances is to produce a distance matrix of the values. This matrix visually displays the distances between points in a way that's easier to read than plotting them individually.

	A	B	C	D
A	0	1	6.32	7.62
B	1	0	6.08	7.28
C	6.32	6.08	0	1.41
D	7.62	7.28	1.41	0

In the distance matrix, the rows and columns represent the data points, in this case A, B, C, and D. The diagonal elements are all zeros because the distance from a point to itself is zero (e.g., the distance from A to A is zero). Since the matrix is symmetric across the diagonal, you don't need both the upper and lower triangles. You can use either one to get all the necessary information although often both are left on the matrix display.

	A	B	C	D
A	0	1	6.32	7.62
B		0	6.08	7.28
C			0	1.41
D				0

This distance matrix is essential for clustering and other data analysis techniques. It provides a clear and concise way to understand the relationships between different points in a dataset, making it easier to identify patterns and groupings. Most data mining software will generate this distance matrix for you, making the process straightforward. Looking over the distance matrix is good practice before applying data mining algorithms.

Review Questions

1. What is clustering, and why use it?
2. Why is distance key in clustering?
3. How does the Pythagorean theorem relate to Euclidean distance?
4. How do you find distance in 2D?
5. Why not use Euclidean distance for binary data?
6. When is Jaccard distance better?
7. What does Mahalanobis distance account for?
8. Why normalize data before clustering?
9. Find Euclidean distance: (3, 4) and (0, 0).
10. Given A(1,2), B(4,6), C(1,5): find pairwise distances and matrix.
11. When do you use Mahalanobis over Euclidean?
12. How does a distance matrix help before clustering?
13. What does a zero in a distance matrix mean?
14. If A is closer to B than C, what does that suggest?

4-3 Normalization and scaling

Learning Outcomes

4-3-1 Understand why we scale or normalize data in data mining.

4-3-2 Know that different units (like pounds vs. kilograms) can change how distances look.

4-3-3 Explain what a Z-score is and why we use it.

4-3-4 See how unscaled data can give misleading results in clustering.

4-3-5 Know that most data mining tools can do normalization for you.

In the previous chapter, we discussed how to normalize data, which involves standardizing it to the standard normal distribution (Z-scores). This process is crucial in data mining to ensure consistent scaling of data. Normalization standardizes the measurement scale, such as inches, dollars, or centimeters, to a standard score to avoid discrepancies in distance calculations.

Consider an example of weight measured in different units. If I weigh 180 lbs and you weigh 160 lbs, the distance between our weights is 20 lbs. If converted to kilograms, 180 lbs is approximately 81.6 kg, and 160 lbs is approximately 72.6 kg, resulting in a distance of 9 kg.

Though the actual difference between our weights remains the same, the numerical distance changes with the unit of measurement. This discrepancy affects the accuracy of distance calculations in data mining, highlighting the importance of normalization.

Without normalization, different units of measurement can distort the true distances between data points. For instance, the difference in weights appears larger in pounds (20) than in kilograms (9), even though it's the same individuals and the same weight difference.

Let's consider a little more complex example considering height and weight measurements (two variables).

First compute distance on measurement scales used

Data in Inches and pounds

Me (66 in,180 lb.)
You (64 in, 160 lb.)

Distance = 20.1

Data in CM and KG

Me (167.6 cm ,81.6 kg)
You (162.6 cm , 72.6 kg)

Distance = 10.3

Without standardizing the data to z scores the distances are very different due to inconsistent measurement scales of English and metric measures. To avoid such inconsistencies, always scale your data to a standard normal distribution before performing any distance calculations. This ensures that all measurements are on the same scale, allowing for accurate and meaningful analysis. After standardization the distances are the same.

Standardize the data and compute distances

Inches and pounds
STANDARDIZED
Mean 171 lb, 64 in (sd 10 lb, 3 in)

CM and KG
STANDARDIZED
Mean 77.6 kg, 162.6 cm (sd 4.5 kg, 7.6 cm)

Me (0.7, 0.9)

You (0, -1.1)

Distance = 2.1

Me (0.7, 0.9)

You (0,   -1.1)

Distance = 2.1

Most data mining software will easily perform normalization and generate distance matrices. This is why dedicated data mining tools are preferred over general statistical software or tools like Excel, which might not handle these tasks as efficiently.

Normalization is crucial in data mining, especially for clustering, which relies on distance calculations. Standardizing data to Z-scores ensures that the measurement scale does not distort the results, providing stable and consistent distances. This foundational step is essential for accurate data analysis and meaningful clustering results.

Review Questions

1. Why do we need to normalize data before comparing it?
2. How does using pounds vs. kilograms change the distance between two weights?
3. What does a Z-score do to a data value?
4. What happens if we skip normalization before clustering?
5. How do Z-scores help us compare different types of data fairly?

4-4 Clustering techniques

Learning Outcomes

4-4-1 Explain what cluster analysis is and why it's useful.

4-4-2 Understand how distance helps group similar data.

4-4-3 Choose meaningful variables for clustering.

4-4-4 Give examples of how clustering is used in real life.

4-4-5 Tell the difference between hierarchical and K-means clustering.

Cluster analysis in data mining refers to techniques of grouping unlabeled data based on distance metrics. In considering the variables to include in your cluster analysis, it's essential to exercise discretion. While you technically could use all available variables, it's often more prudent to be selective. For instance, with a smaller dataset containing only a handful of quantitative variables, utilizing all of them might make sense. However, in more extensive datasets with numerous variables, such as a hundred or more, it's wiser to narrow down your selection to a more manageable number, say six or so.

When deciding which variables to include, focus on those that offer valuable insights into the structure of your data. For instance, if you're analyzing customer traits, variables like gender and age could be pivotal in identifying distinct customer groups for targeted marketing strategies. It's crucial to exercise discretion when selecting variables for cluster analysis. Avoid including irrelevant or inconsequential variables, such as ID numbers or irrelevant demographic data. Instead, focus on variables that provide meaningful insights into the underlying structure of your data.

Remember, cluster analysis hinges on the concept of similarity, which is quantified using mathematical distance metrics. While the Euclidean distance metric is commonly used, there are alternative metrics tailored to specific data types, such as binary data.

In essence, cluster analysis serves as a powerful exploratory tool for uncovering hidden patterns and structures within your data. By judiciously selecting variables and employing appropriate distance metrics, you can extract valuable insights that drive informed decision-making and further analysis.

Cluster analysis finds myriad applications across various domains, particularly in business and biological research. For instance, in retail, businesses may employ cluster analysis to identify buying patterns by clustering items that customers frequently purchase together. This information can then inform marketing strategies, such as bundling related products into attractive deals. In the realm of finance, cluster analysis can be instrumental in identifying stocks that exhibit similar behavior, such as those that tend to rise and fall in tandem. By clustering such stocks, investors can gain insights into market trends and correlations, aiding in portfolio management and risk assessment.

Visualizing clusters often involves representing them graphically, as demonstrated in the accompanying illustration.

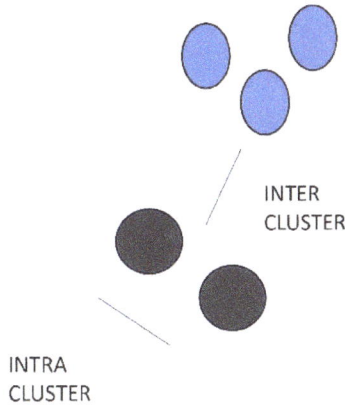

Here, clusters are denoted by distinct colors, with each point representing a data point. The distance between points within a cluster, as well as between clusters, is crucial in cluster analysis. Ideally, clusters should exhibit tight cohesion internally, with data points closely grouped together within the same cluster. Conversely, the distance between clusters should be maximized, ensuring clear demarcation between distinct clusters. In essence, the goal is to minimize intra-cluster distance while maximizing inter-cluster distance, thereby delineating meaningful clusters within the dataset.

There are two primary methodologies for clustering that we'll delve into: hierarchical and K-means. Hierarchical clustering groups data points together in a hierarchical manner, forming a structured agglomerated cluster, while K-means clustering creates separate clusters, akin to individual bubbles.

Review Questions

1. What is cluster analysis used for?
2. Why should you choose your variables carefully?
3. What does Euclidean distance measure?
4. Give one example of how a business might use clustering.

4-5 Hierarchical clustering

Learning Outcomes

4-5-1 Say what hierarchical clustering is.

4-5-2 Know that we start with each point in its own group.

4-5-3 Tell how we find which points are closest.

4-5-4 Understand how small groups are joined to make bigger ones.

4-5-5 Read a dendrogram (a tree diagram) to see how groups were formed.

4-5-6 Know some good and bad things about this method.

Let's begin with hierarchical clustering. In hierarchical clustering, also known as agglomerative clustering, the process starts with each data point as its own cluster. As the algorithm progresses, it merges similar clusters together, creating a hierarchical structure.

To illustrate hierarchical clustering, consider the following example. We have six data points labeled A, B, C, D, E, and F, each with X and Y coordinates. These points are initially plotted on a graph, as shown. Initially, each point constitutes its own cluster.

C 1	N 2	N 3
Obs	x	y
A	1	2
B	2	2
C	3	8
D	4	9
E	5	4
F	6	7

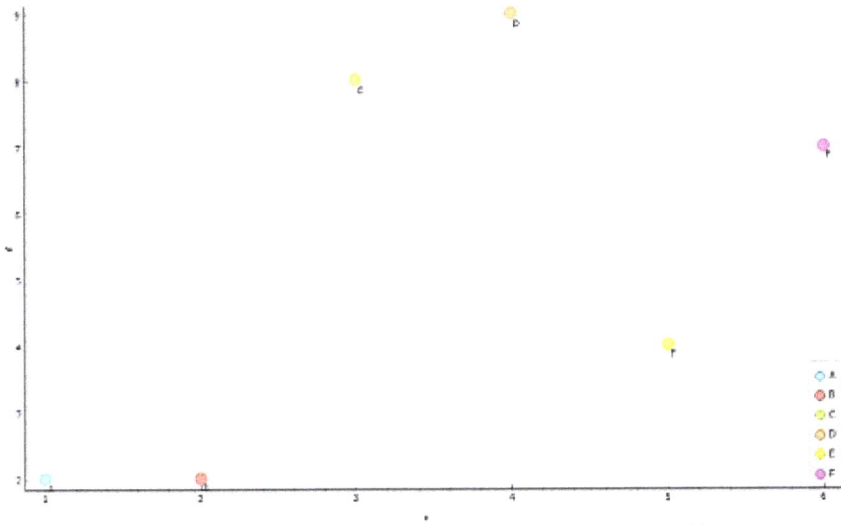

Next, we calculate the distance matrix, a crucial step in hierarchical clustering. This matrix depicts the distances between all pairs of points. In this example, the distances are illustrated visually by highlighting the strongest distances, aiding in the clustering process.

	A	B	C	D	E	F
A		1.414	6.403	7.681	4.583	7.141
B	1.414		6.164	7.348	3.742	6.481
C	6.403	6.164		1.732	4.583	3.317
D	7.681	7.348	1.732		5.196	3.000
E	4.583	3.742	4.583	5.196		3.317
F	7.141	6.481	3.317	3.000	3.317	

Although the data in this example is not standardized, it is on the same measurement scale of the coordinate axis. Note in real-world applications, it's advisable to work with standardized data to ensure accurate clustering results. However, for illustrative purposes, this toy dataset suffices.

Now, using the distance matrix, we proceed with the hierarchical clustering algorithm, iteratively merging clusters based on their proximity until a hierarchical structure is formed. This hierarchical representation captures the relationships between data points, facilitating pattern identification and analysis.

In hierarchical clustering, the first step involves identifying the closest points. These are the points with the smallest distances between them. In our example, points A to B and C to D have relatively small distances compared to the others, so they form clusters. At this stage, each point starts as its own cluster, and the closest pairs are merged to form new clusters. In this case, A and B form one cluster, while C and D form another, leaving E and F as individual clusters.

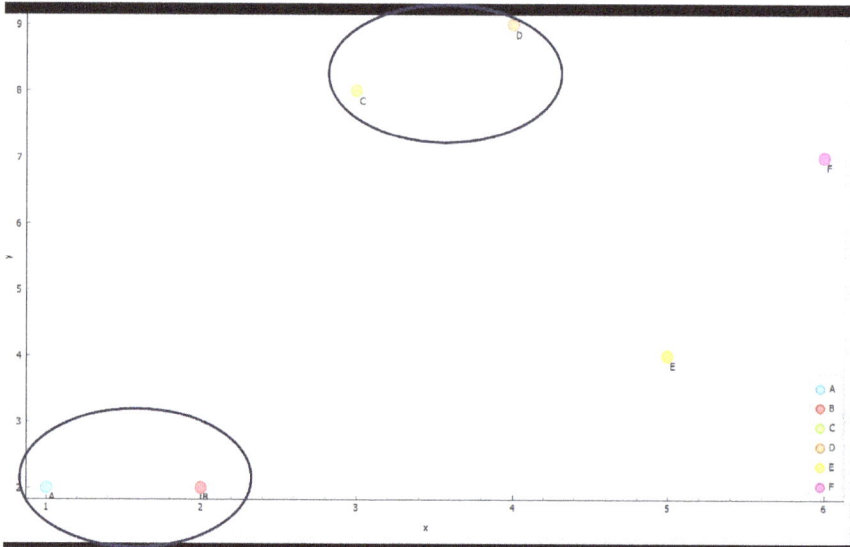

Now, let's talk about calculating distances. Initially, distances between in-dividual points are derived from the distance matrix. But as clusters are formed, we need to calculate distances between clusters as well. This intro-duces the concept of linkage. Linkage refers to the method used to deter-mine the distance between clusters.

There are different linkage methods, such as single linkage and complete linkage. Single linkage seeks to minimize the distance between the closest points of two clusters. In our example, single linkage would consider the distance between the closest points of the AB cluster and the CD cluster.

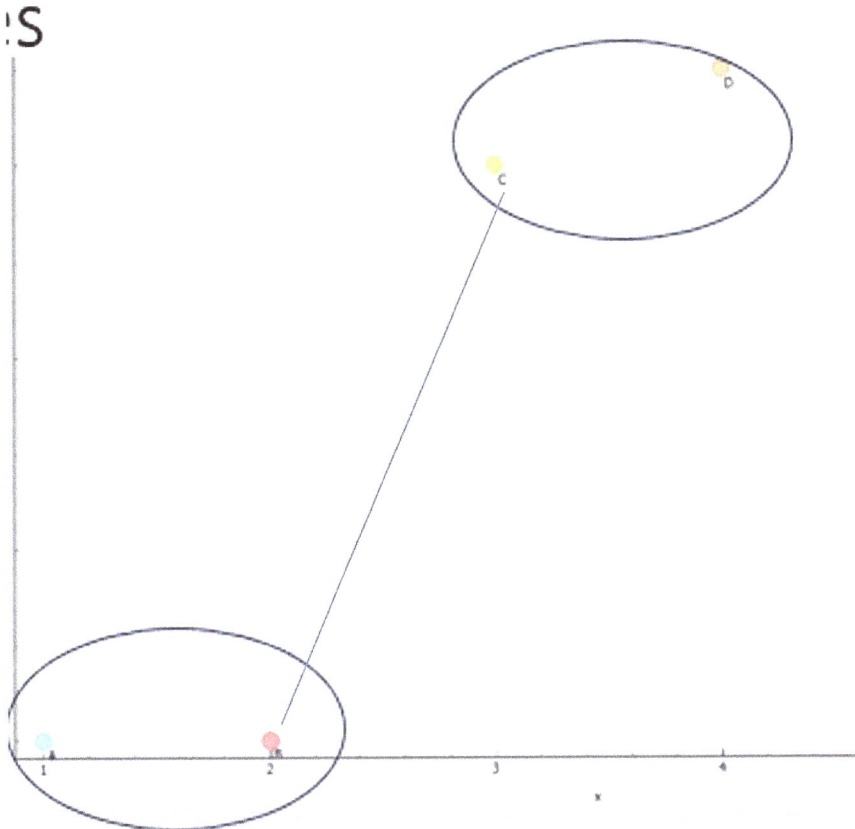

On the other hand, complete linkage measures the distance between the furthest points of two clusters. This would involve considering the distance between the furthest points of the AB cluster and the CD cluster.

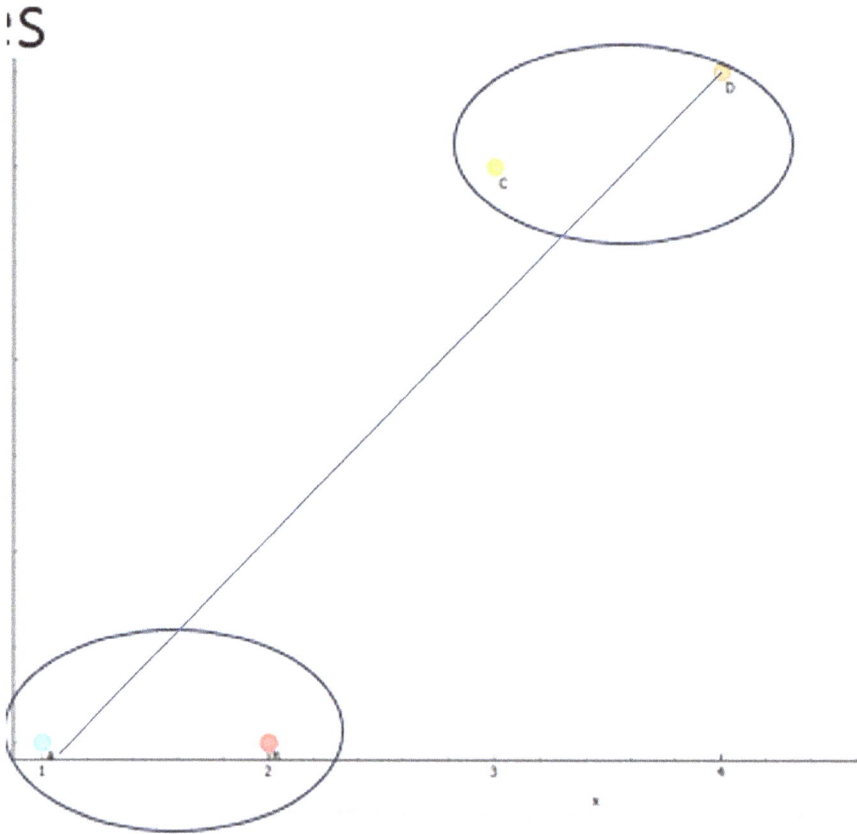

Moving on, there's another linkage method called average linkage, which is generally recommended. This method tends to provide more reliable results in hierarchical clustering. It's considered a sensible choice for most scenarios.

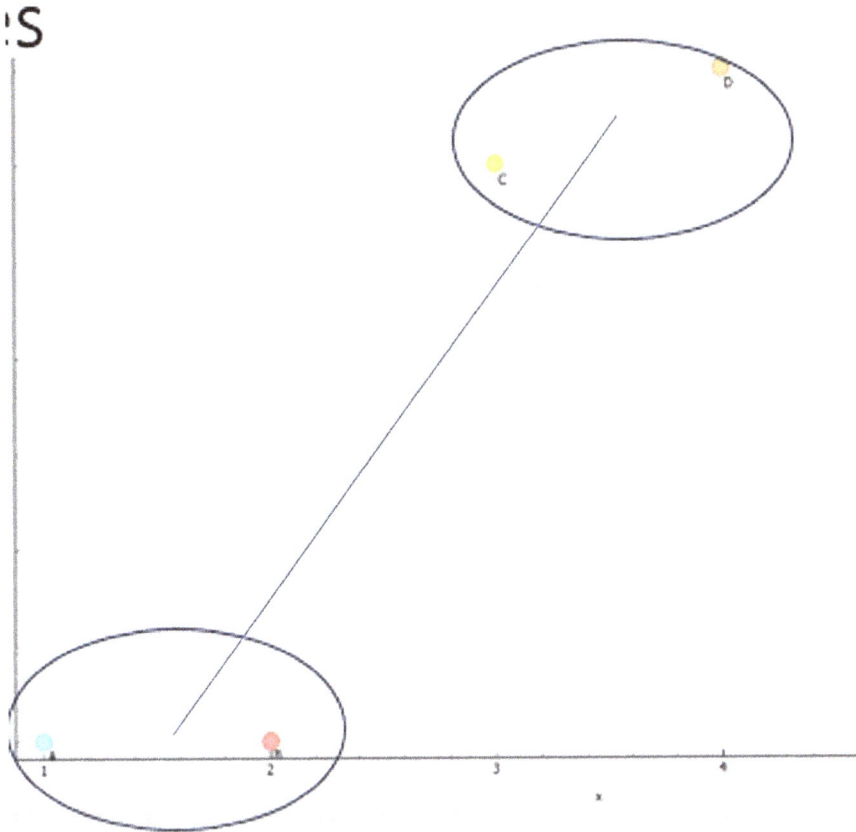

Another method worth mentioning is Ward's method (often abbreviated as "WS"). Although it's widely used, this method can be complex and may require a deeper understanding to implement effectively. Ward's method will not be illustrated here.

As with other aspects of hierarchical clustering, the software you're using will typically offer options to select the desired linkage metric. When in doubt, average linkage is a safe choice, but it's also valuable to explore different methods to understand their impact on your results. Each linkage method has its advantages and is suited for different types of data and clustering objectives. It's important to choose the appropriate linkage method based on the specific characteristics of your dataset and the goals of your analysis. Keep in mind that the choice of linkage method can sometimes significantly influence the outcomes of hierarchical clustering. It's essential to note that linkage is specific to hierarchical clustering as it is a result of the agglomerative process – other data mining techniques do not use linkage metrics.

Returning to our example, the choice of linkage metric for this example doesn't significantly affect the clustering outcome. In our illustration, after the first two clusters are formed next the smallest distance using single linkage is now F to D so point F is joined (agglomerated) to the cluster containing C and D.

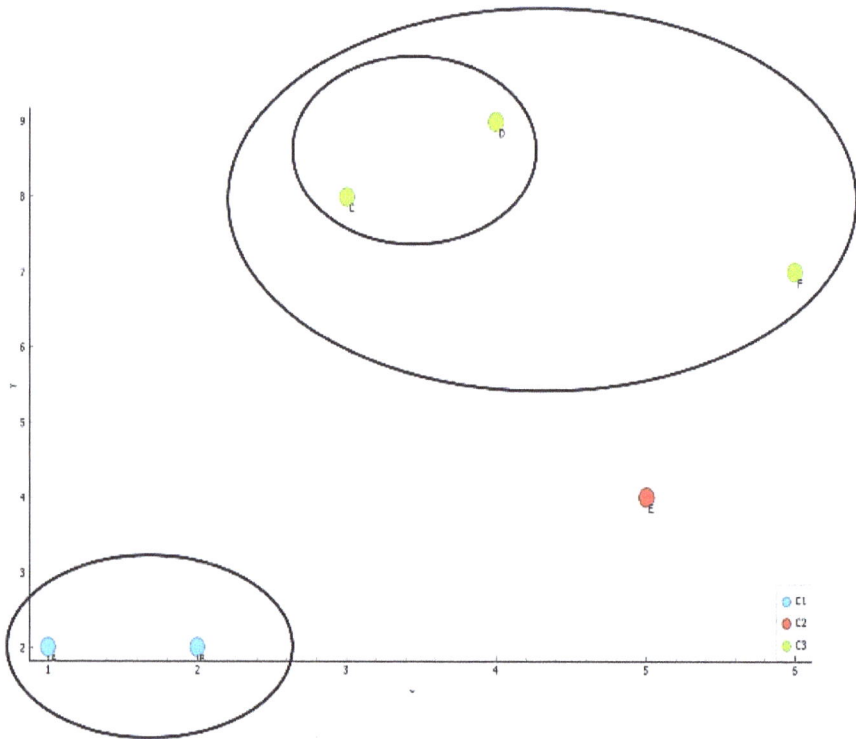

Next, we move on to clustering the remaining points. You can observe that the next logical step is to cluster this point E (now in red, recolored from yellow in first graph above) with its closest cluster, as it's farther away from the others. As we join it with the nearest cluster, we create a larger cluster.

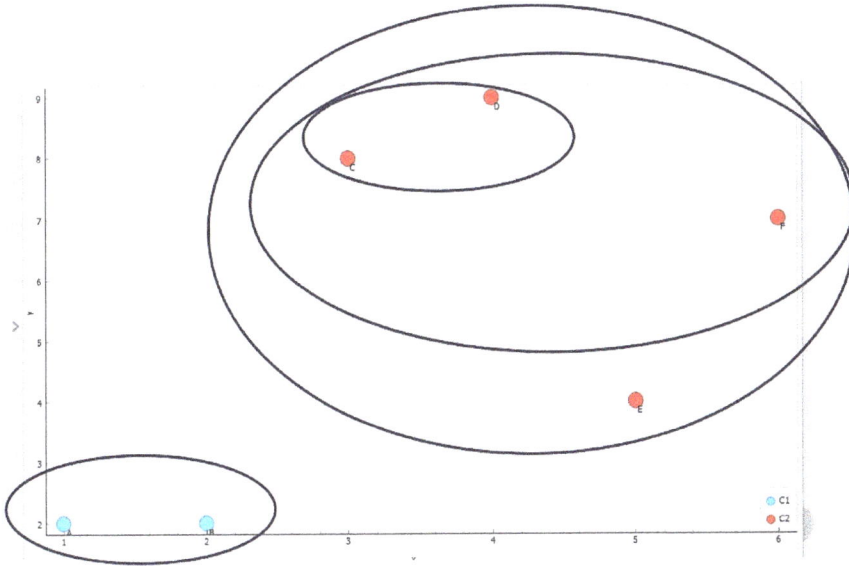

This process continues until we have one big cluster containing all points, marking the completion of our hierarchical clustering. At this point the only thing left to do is join all the clusters for the final agglomeration.

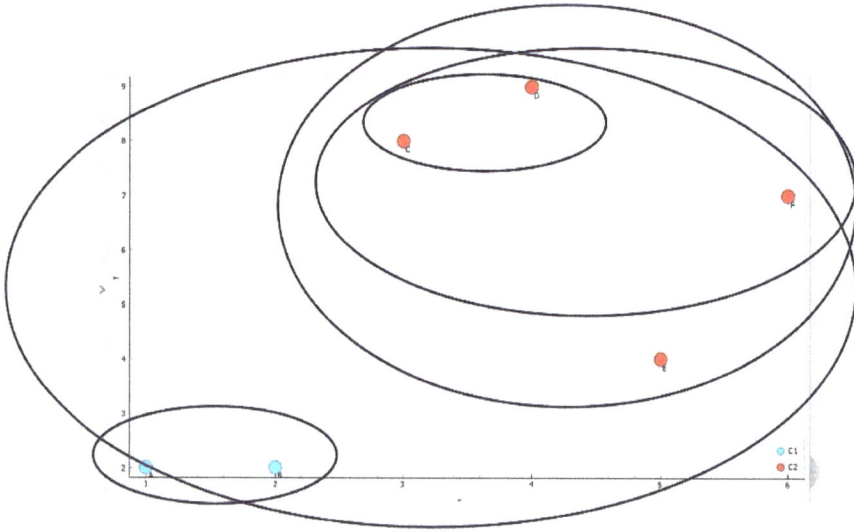

To visualize the hierarchical clustering process, we use a tool called a dendrogram. This graphical representation helps us understand hierarchical clustering better than the illustration graphs above in the example. Each step of the merging process is illustrated in the dendrogram. For instance, the initial clusters A, B, C, and D are depicted, followed by the subsequent merging of points until we have one unified cluster. While dendrograms may seem complex at first, they become easier to interpret with practice.

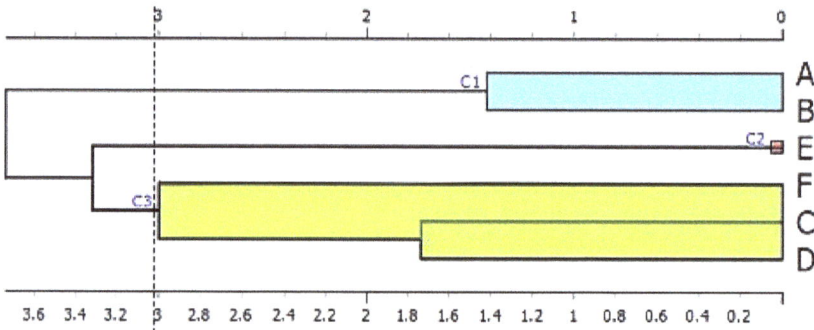

Dendrograms can be particularly useful for identifying patterns or groupings within your data, such as different product categories. In the dendrogram, the axis measures the distances between clusters, highlighting the proximity of different data points. While some results may be easily interpreted, others can be perplexing.

Overall, hierarchical clustering offers a straightforward approach to understanding the structure of your data and uncovering meaningful insights. Hierarchical clustering can yield dendrograms that are both insightful and, at times, convoluted. Since it's an exploratory method, there's no definitive right or wrong outcome. One drawback of hierarchical clustering is its occasional difficulty in result interpretation. Despite some visually appealing outcomes, there are instances where the results might seem odd or uninformative. Additionally, due to its computational demands, hierarchical clustering could strain older computer systems, although this is less of an issue with modern technology. Moreover, with large datasets, the output can become unwieldy, complicating dendrogram results.

> **Review Questions**
>
> 1. What is hierarchical clustering?
> 2. What happens at the beginning of the clustering process?
> 3. What is a distance matrix?
> 4. What does "linkage" mean?
> 5. What is a dendrogram?
> 6. What is one good thing about hierarchical clustering?
> 7. What is one bad thing about hierarchical clustering?
> 8. Why do we sometimes change the scale of the data before clustering?

4-6 K Means clustering

Learning Outcomes

4-6-1 Say what K-means clustering is and why we use it.

4-6-2 List the basic steps of how K-means works.

4-6-3 Explain how to choose the best number of clusters (K).

4-6-4 Tell how K-means and hierarchical clustering are different.

4-6-5 Use tools like Orange to try out K-means clustering.

4-6-6 Understand how the clusters change as the algorithm runs.

Hierarchical clustering seeks to agglomerate and join clusters creating one structure for the entire dataset. An alternative method is K means clustering. The methodology for K means clustering is to create clusters which do not join the entire dataset together but divide the data into distinguished clusters which have independence from other clusters. K means is a method for clustering unlabeled data and groups it based on similarities into non-overlapping clusters. Like hierarchical clustering similarity is measured with distance metrics.

First, you set a value for K, which represents the number of clusters you want to create. Next, K-means randomly places centroids within the data. Then, it computes the distance from each point to these centroids, reassigning points to the nearest centroid. This process repeats iteratively, with centroids recalculated based on the mean values of the data points assigned to them. This continues until the centroids stabilize, and the clusters remain unchanged.

To illustrate, imagine an unlabeled dataset featuring age and salary data. Since there are no predefined labels, we turn to unsupervised learning methods like clustering to find order in the data. Upon plotting the data, it becomes apparent that there are three distinct clusters.

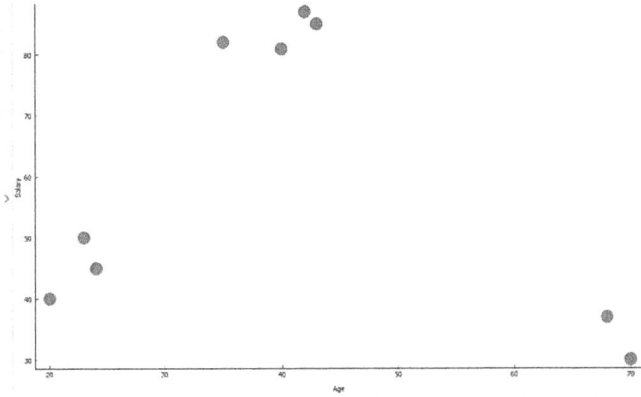

Without a scatter plot to guide us, we could use a technique called a scree plot to determine the optimal value of K. This is the same plot used in principal components analysis (see previous chapter). This involves examining the "elbow" point in the plot to identify the most suitable number of clusters.

Here's the same plot again, showing what appears to be three distinct clusters. Plots like this are available for the K-means clustering process using a tool like Orange. To start the process the number of clusters is inputted in the software. Initially, it might look a bit complex, but let's break it down. The dots represent the data points, while the squares indicate the centroids. These centroids are randomly positioned on the plot, a step characteristic of K-means. In this example, the centroids are initially scattered across the data space.

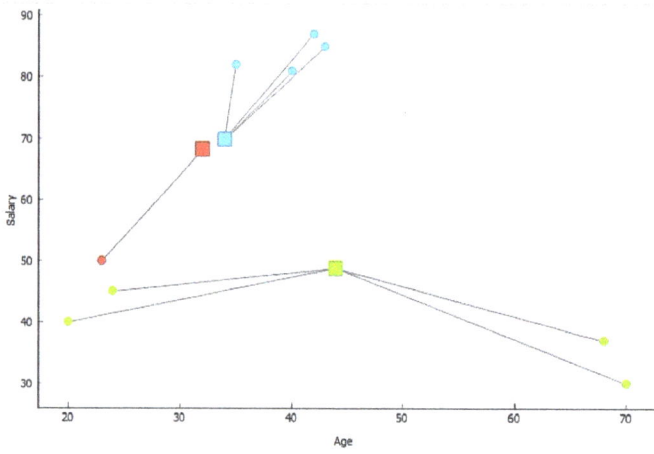

Next, the algorithm computes the distances between each point and the centroids. Based on these distances, each point is assigned to the nearest centroid, forming initial clusters. Then, the centroids are recalculated based on the mean positions of the points assigned to them.

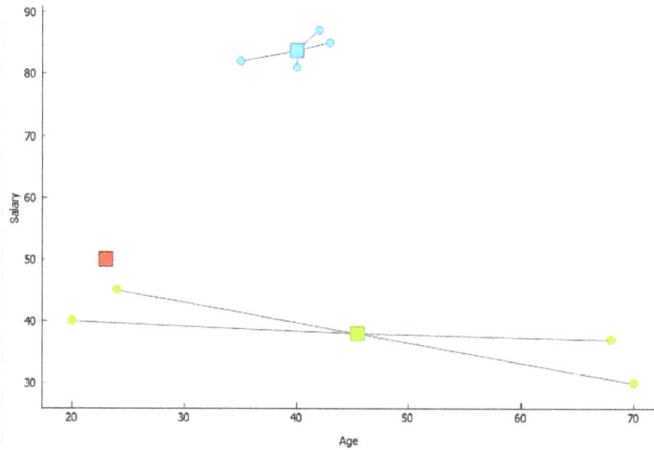

As the centroids move to new positions, the membership of points may change. Points are reassigned to the centroid that is now closest to them.

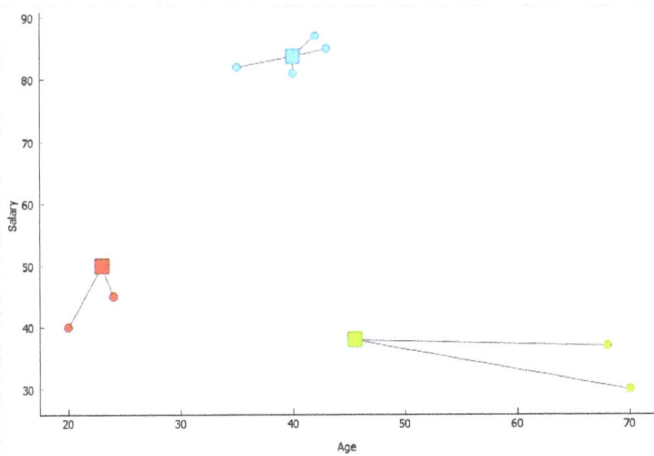

This process iterates, with centroids and cluster assignments recalculated until the clusters stabilize and centroids no longer shift significantly.

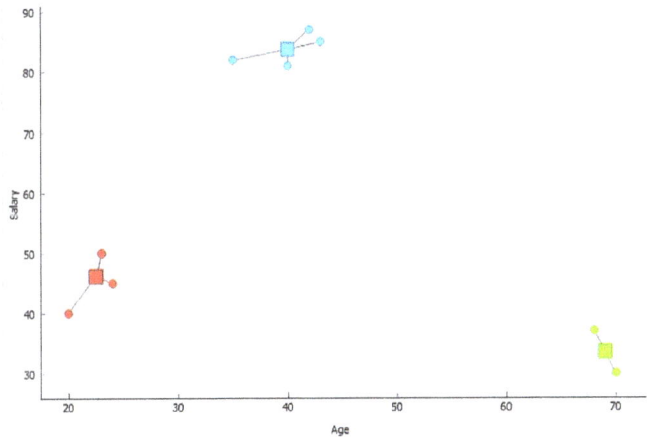

So, while the data points remain static, the centroids dynamically adjust their positions to best represent the clusters, resulting in an optimal clustering solution. The duplicate pic below shows nothing changes.

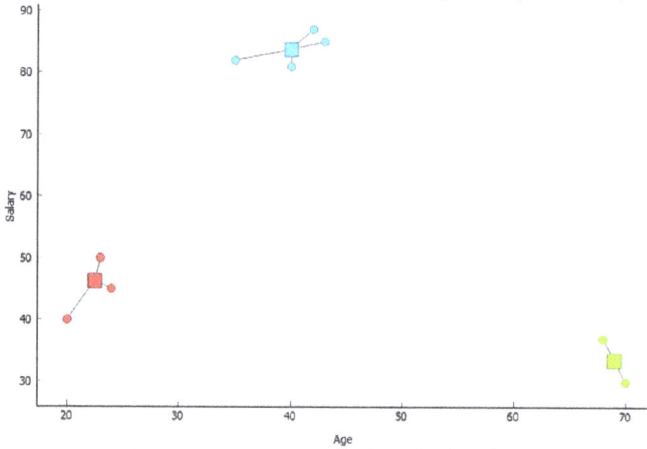

So, let's wrap up the K-means clustering process to recap. Initially, the centroids are randomly positioned. Then, points are assigned to the closest centroids. Following this, centroids are recalculated and adjusted based on the assigned points. This continues until a stable state is reached. When this process stabilizes and no further changes occur, you've reached a stable state with your clusters.

Determining how many clusters

Determining the optimal number of clusters is a crucial aspect of k means cluster analysis (in hierarchical clustering this is a non-issue). In some cases, like the example above, the clusters may be evident. However, this isn't always the case. Typically, you won't have less than 3 or more than six or eight clusters, as having too few or too many clusters can be impractical.

To decide on the number of clusters, you can use a method called a scree plot. This plot, generated by software, displays the variance in the data. By reducing dimensionality, like principal components analysis, you can determine the number of clusters needed to capture most of the data's variability. Essentially, you're looking for a point where adding more clusters doesn't significantly improve the explanation of variance.

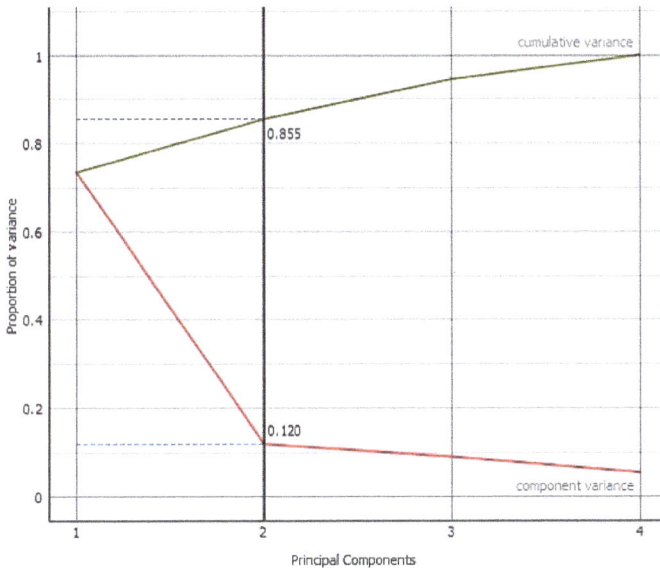

Another method is using silhouette scores. These scores evaluate how well each data point fits within its cluster, quantifying the cohesion within clusters and separation from neighboring clusters. Silhouette scores provide a numerical measure of cluster quality, helping you assess the effectiveness of your clustering algorithm.

For each data point, an individual silhouette score is the difference between its distance to its own cluster's center (B) and the average distance to all points in the nearest neighboring cluster (A). This difference is then divided by the maximum of A and B. Silhouette scores range from -1 to 1, with a score of 1 indicating a perfect match, 0 indicating a point on the cluster boundary, and -1 indicating a misclassification.

The overall silhouette score, which is the average of silhouette scores for all data points, is crucial. It helps determine the optimal number of clusters (K). The higher the silhouette score, the better the clustering. In practice, you compute silhouette scores for different values of K and select the value that maximizes the overall silhouette score. This is doing using software which has this specialized computation available.

In the same example used for the k means illustration above, the silhouette scores for K = 2, 3, 4, 5, 6, 7, and 8 were computed using software. The highest silhouette score, corresponding to K = 3, suggests that three clusters best fit the data. This approach provides an alternative to the scree plot method for determining the optimal number of clusters.

Silhouette Scores

2	0.610
3	**0.852**
4	0.686
5	0.529
6	0.354
7	0.299
8	0.321

So, that's cluster analysis in a nutshell. It's not overly complicated, but it's highly exploratory. When to use K-means versus hierarchical clustering depends on your goals, preferences, and dataset characteristics. You can use both techniques—there's no rule against it and in fact the results together are more powerful than using either technique exclusively. Generally, K-means performs better with large datasets because it's more efficient and doesn't generate unwieldy dendrograms like hierarchical clustering does. K-means tends to offer clearer cluster separation, which can be visually appealing. And that's the theory behind cluster analysis—a very helpful technique for exploring data to find meaningful groupings.

Review Questions

1. What is K-means clustering, and what kind of data is it used for?
2. What are the main steps in the K-means clustering process?
3. How is similarity between data points measured in K-means clustering?
4. What does a centroid do in K-means, and how does it move?
5. How can we find the best number of clusters in K-means?
6. When should you use K-means instead of hierarchical clustering?

Chapter 5

Classification Analysis

5-1 Introduction

Learning Outcomes

5-1-1 Say what classification is and why it's important.

5-1-2 Tell the difference between classification and clustering.

5-1-3 Know what kind of data you need to do classification.

5-1-4 Understand the steps to build a classification model.

5-1-5 Know why it's important to mix up (randomize) your data before splitting it.

5-1-6 Give real-life examples where classification is used.

Classification is a pivotal topic, and very important technique in Data Mining. The primary objective of classification is to construct models capable of predicting the class label of new data, leveraging patterns and relationships identified in the original (training) data. In machine learning terminology this is referred to as supervised learning.

This necessitates having a column of data containing pre-existing categories or labels, unlike clustering, where such labels are not required. Data can be fundamentally quantitative or qualitative, with quantitative data being discrete or continuous. Clustering, aka unsupervised learning, can be performed solely on quantitative data, without the need for qualitative variables as it requires no labels on the original data.

To perform classification prediction using data, it's essential to have qualitative data variables. Specifically, you need a categorical variable with a finite set of values that can serve as labels. Good labels typically include binary outcomes like "yes" and "no," or discreet quantitative or qualitative variables. Examples could be colors, types of pets, or other categories with a limited number of options. Quantitative data can be binned to create classification useful qualitative variables. For instance, you could group income into categories like "under $50,000," "$50,000 to $80,000," and "over $80,000."

Basics of classification

When developing a classification model, regardless of the specific type, the process generally involves common steps. First, you select the label you want to predict as the outcome variable. Then, you randomly divide the data into two parts: training data and test data. Once you've got your data split, the next step is to develop the model using the training data. Finally, you use the test data on the model to test its accuracy. This testing phase is crucial as you don't want to use a model that does not perform accurate classification.

When you're developing a model, you typically split your original data into two parts: training data and test data. A common split is 80% for training and 20% for testing, but there's flexibility here. There's no strict rule, but the key is to avoid bias and the selection of data needs to be randomized. Let me share a cautionary tale: once, in a class working with a student, we worked with Iris data, but the dataset was pre-sorted by flower type and wasn't randomized, and the test/train split was based on rows so that all of one flower type ended up in the training data and all of others in the test

– do not do this ever. So, remember, always randomize your data before splitting it!

Applications of classification

One of the appeals in learning how to do classification is the number of applications classification analysis has. One classic example is detecting spam emails where the label data is span/not spam. Medically, classification can be incredibly useful for diagnosing diseases. Picture having a database of symptoms matched with the corresponding disease outcomes. Models can be made based on this predicting probability of disease. Another use of classification is credit risk assessment. Whether it's evaluating mortgage applications or car loans, the goal is to classify them as low or high risk based on various factors. Another practical application is in image classification. You can feed pictures of cats and dogs into a model to predict whether a new image is of a cat or a dog. This demonstrates how classification techniques can be applied in various contexts and prove useful in many scenarios.

These applications form the foundation for machine learning and artificial intelligence. While data mining focuses on analyzing data and identifying patterns, machine learning involves training computers to learn independently.

Review Questions

1. What is classification?
2. How is classification different from clustering?
3. What kind of data do you need to do classification?
4. What are the basic steps to make a classification model?
5. Why is it bad to split your data without randomizing it?
6. Name three real-world things classification can help with.
7. Can you use number data (quantitative data) in classification? How?
8. Why do we test the model after training it?

5-2 Probability basics

Learning Outcomes

5-2-1 Understand what probability means and how to write it.

5-2-2 Explain what conditional probability is (like $P(B \mid A)$).

5-2-3 Know the difference between false positives and false negatives.

5-2-4 Use conditional probability to understand classification test results.

5-2-5 Understand why errors happen in classification models.

5-2-6 Recognize and read a confusion matrix to check model accuracy.

Before delving into classification and how the algorithms work, it's important to talk a little about probability because classification is based on probability. Understanding probability basics is essential for grasping classification techniques. Probability, denoted as P(A), represents the likelihood of an event A occurring. It's essentially the frequency of that event happening. For instance, if 100 items are sold and 10 of them are coffee, the probability of selling coffee is 10 out of 100, or 0.1. We often express probability as a decimal, though fractions or percentages work too.

If we make things a little more complicated, we can talk about relations between events A and B and how these events impact each other. If event A occurs before event B and impacts the probability of event B occurring, we say event B is dependent on event A. This dependency creates a situation we call conditional probability. To state this in probability terms we say that 'the probability of B given A' is P (B | A). In the realm of classification, this concept becomes vital for assessing model accuracy.

Now, let's apply this basic probability concept to a real-world scenario. Medical testing serves as a perfect example. Consider a pre-employment drug screening—a practice that might not be as common nowadays but was once widespread. These tests aim to determine whether someone uses drugs. However, here's the catch: tests aren't infallible. They can yield false positives or false negatives. To better understand this, let's look at a hypothetical scenario with test results in one column and actual drug usage in the other.

	Positive test result	Negative test result
Actual drug use	20	10
No actual drug use	5	65

Out of the group, 20 individuals test positive for drug use, which aligns with their actual drug usage—this is expected. However, there are also 10 individuals who test negative despite being actual drug users. Clearly, this is not ideal. Conditional probability can describe and quantify these errors. We call the error of a negative test when the true result is positive a false negative result. In probability notation this is quantified as P(Negative test

result | Actual drug use) is a **false negative**. According to the data this equals
10/30 or 0.33 (33%). The probability statement here is read the probability
of a negative test result given actual drug use, note the denominator is 30
because the condition is actual drug use.

	Positive test result	Negative test result
Actual drug use	20	10
No actual drug use	5	65

Conversely, 65 individuals test negative, and indeed, they don't use drugs.
So, this result is expected. But we encounter another issue: five individuals
test positive, but they do not use drugs. Conditional probability can describe
this as P(Positive test result | No actual drug use). This is called a false
positive. Such a situation of testing positive when the true result should be
negative is a false positive. Computationally this equals 5/70 or 0.07 (7%).

	Positive test result	Negative test result
Actual drug use	20	10
No actual drug use	5	65

You see, in classification modeling, minimizing errors is crucial. Yet, achieving perfection is nearly impossible, even in medical testing. Remember the
recent COVID-19 tests? They sometimes produced false positives or false

negatives. A false positive occurs when you test positive despite not using drugs. Conversely, a false negative happens when you test negative despite being a drug user. This highlights the importance of conditional probability, particularly when interpreting test results.

Classification errors

In classification, the error analysis in the above example is heavily used in determining how accurate a model is. Let's say we have data with labels A or B, and we aim to develop a model to classify data into these groups.

Now, let's swap out the medical example for a classification scenario with groups A and B by simply relabeling the axis (the data is the same as it is just for illustration). This setup serves as our foundation for evaluating modeling accuracy—a critical concern in classification.

	Predicted class A	Predicted class B
Actual class A	20	10
Actual class B	5	65

To assess model performance, the table analysis of errors above is referred to as a confusion matrix. From this matrix you can determine correct results, false positives, and false negatives. While accuracy has a few more metrics, these are the basic assessments of model accuracy. Evey classification algorithm is assessed for accuracy using a confusion matrix.

Review Questions

1. What is probability? Give an example.
2. What does $P(B \mid A)$ mean in words?
3. What is a false positive? What is a false negative?
4. How can we use conditional probability to describe testing errors?
5. What does a confusion matrix show us?
6. Why can't classification models be perfect?
7. Why is it important to understand probability when doing classification?

5-3 Logistic regression

Learning Outcomes

5-3-1 Understand the difference between linear and logistic regression.
5-3-2 Explain when and why logistic regression is used for binary outcomes.
5-3-3 Describe odds, odds ratios, and the logit function.
5-3-4 Interpret the logistic regression equation and predicted probabilities.
5-3-5 Use logistic regression to classify binary outcomes.
5-3-6 Evaluate model performance with a confusion matrix.

Logistic regression occupies a unique space as it functions as both a statistical and classification model. Understanding how logistic regression works a foundation is for understanding how classification models generally work. Unlike linear regression, where the outcome is continuous, logistic regression deals with binary outcomes, typically represented as yes or no, 0 or 1.

To differentiate, let's briefly touch on linear regression. In linear regression, you might have studied the relationship between two continuous quantitative variables like income and years of education.

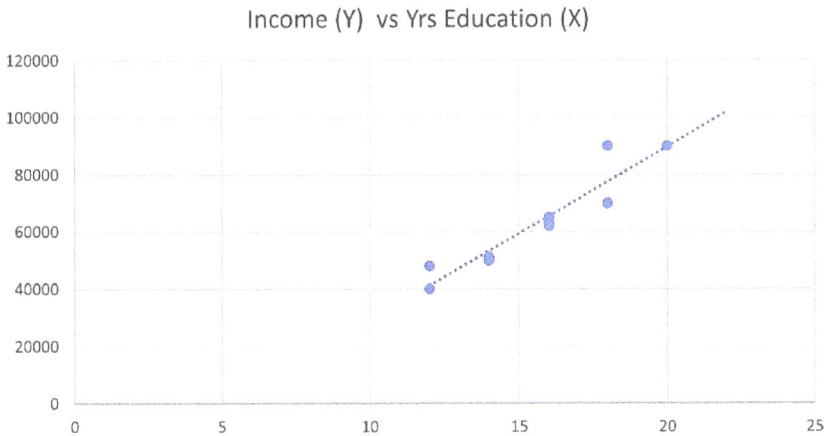

Income (Y) vs Yrs Education (X)

The graph illustrates a linear pattern, suggesting that as education level increases, income tends to rise as well. With linear regression, you'd use the familiar formula y = mx + b to create a best-fit line, allowing for predictions of income based on education levels. In the example provided, using software we obtain an equation representing the line, income = 6050 * education - 31,000. The slope of the line tells us how income changes with each additional year of education, which, in this case, is $6,050.

While we won't delve too deeply into it, the concept of using data to fit a mathematical model is essential and the foundation of much of statistics. However, it's important to note that linear regression is suitable for predicting continuous variables, like income, but not binary outcomes, which are more relevant in classification tasks. Despite this distinction, the underlying idea remains the same across prediction models. But for classification, where we're interested in binary outcomes (yes or no, 0 or 1), we need a different approach. This is where logistic regression comes in.

Logistic regression, unlike linear regression, is tailored for binary outcomes. It works with a binary Y variable, representing outcomes as either 0 or 1. For instance, in a scenario where we predict whether someone is over the age of 16 (1 for yes, 0 for no) based on their height, logistic regression is the appropriate tool. In this data we have a categorical variable instead of a linear pattern.

Height, in	Adult (>16)	Adult_Binary
60	Y	1
47	N	0
36	N	0
66	Y	1
61	N	0
57	N	0
72	Y	1
65	Y	1
60	N	0
68	Y	1

Would we use linear regression for this? Looking at the bivariate scatterplot to use linear regression you should see a linear pattern. In this plot this is not the pattern.

Adult Status vs Height

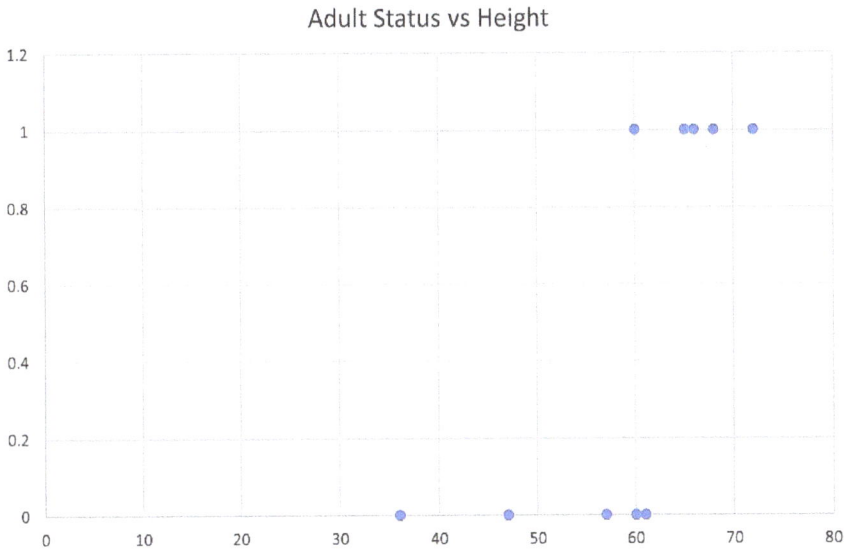

We need a different approach. This calls for logistic regression. Unlike linear regression, logistic regression is tailored for binary outcomes, making it perfect for scenarios like this.

Odds ratio

Before diving into logistic regression, let's touch on another probability concept: odds ratio. Simply put, an odds ratio is just another way to express probability. It's calculated as the probability of an event (p) over the probability of its complement (1-p). Recall the complement is everything else in the sample space except the event and probability of the event plus probability of the event's complement equals 1.

$$Odds = \frac{p}{1-p}$$

For example, if the probability of winning is 1 out of 3 games, the odds of winning would be 1 to 2, as it represents the ratio between winning and not winning. So, odds ratios offer an alternative perspective on probabilities, providing valuable insights into various scenarios.

$$Odds = \frac{1/3}{1-1/3} = \frac{1/3}{2/3} = \frac{1}{2} \; written \; as \; 1:2$$

Logit metric

In logistic regression, the Y variable takes on what's known as a logit metric. If we take the natural logarithm of the odds ratio this is the "log odds" or logit metric

$$\ln \frac{p}{1-P}$$

The logit metric ranges from negative infinity (if p=0) to positive infinity (if p =1) and is equal to zero when p=0.5.

Logistic model

Now, the logistic regression model resembles linear regression at first glance, with one key difference: the Y variable is replaced by this logit ratio. Let's compare the mathematical equations for one variable input. In linear regression the y (dependent variable) is continuous and normally distributed. In logistic regression the y variable is binary, and the model is doing a probability prediction.

$$\text{Simple regression: one input variable}$$
$$y = \beta_0 + \beta_1 x$$

$$\text{Logistic regression: one input variable}$$
$$\ln \frac{p}{1-P} = \beta_0 + \beta_1 x$$

In summary, while linear regression deals with a continuous and normally distributed Y variable, logistic regression focuses on a binary Y variable.

In linear regression, your outcome (Y) is continuous, while in logistic regression, your outcome is binary (either 0 or 1). The logistic ratio in logistic regression gives you a probability estimate, which falls somewhere between 0 and 1. Mathematically p can be found as described below:

Solve for p $\ln \frac{p}{1-P} = \beta_0 + \beta_1 x$

(algebra details can be filled in)

$$\text{predicted p} = \frac{e^{(\beta_0 + \beta_1 x)}}{1 + e^{(\beta_0 + \beta_1 x)}}$$

This is the logistic function which gives the relation between p and the explanatory variable.

Logistic regression example

So, if we create a model using the example above, depending on where this probability lies, you can infer whether it's closer to the "adult" or "child" category. First use software to get the model parameters and create the model.

Model

$$\ln\frac{p}{1-P}=\beta_0 + \beta_1 x$$

Model parameters fitted by software

$$\ln\frac{p}{1-P}=\text{-38} + \text{0.62} * height$$

Height, in	Adult_Binary
60	1
47	0
36	0
66	1
61	0
57	0
72	1
65	1
60	0
68	1

Once the model is produced It can be solved for p and used to predict outcomes (review good technique in a precalculus book on solving logarithmic equations for details).

Height, in	Adult_Binary	p pred
60	1	0.310026
47	0	0.000142
36	0	1.55E-07
66	1	0.948826
61	0	0.455121
57	0	0.065375
72	1	0.998695
65	1	0.908877
60	0	0.310026
68	1	0.984632

$$p = \frac{e^{(-38 + 0.62 * height)}}{1 + e^{(-38 + 0.62 * height)}}$$

In this result are the predicted probabilities (likelihoods) based on the height values given the model. For example, the tallest person at 72 inches has a predicted adult probability of 0.99, meaning they're almost certainly an adult. Conversely, someone who's 47 inches tall has an extremely small probability of being an adult.

Next, we can classify as binary outcomes using these predicted probabilities whether someone is a child or adult based on height. For this example, let's use the classification criteria if the predicted probability (p) is less than 0.5, we classify the individual as a child; otherwise, as an adult

Height, in	Adult_Binary	p pred	Predicted binary
60	1	0.310026	0
47	0	0.000142	0
36	0	1.55E-07	0
66	1	0.948826	1
61	0	0.455121	0
57	0	0.065375	0
72	1	0.998695	1
65	1	0.908877	1
60	0	0.310026	0
68	1	0.984632	1

Finally, it is now clear that logistic regression Is considered a classification model (albeit also a statistical model) because it does predict categorical classifications on labelled data (here adult yes/no). As a side, there's a bit of a distinction between data mining and formal statistical analysis. Not all aspects of data analytics qualify as traditional statistics. To truly become a statistician, one needs to dive deep into the mathematical foundations. However, many techniques in data analytics don't require that level of mathematical rigor and are not formal statistics. Logistic regression, however, straddles both realms. It's a staple in upper-level stats courses and finds practical application in data mining due to its simplicity and effectiveness in illustrating classification concepts.

So, in this teaching example with only 10 data points, there was no split of the data into training and testing sets as this is not a big enough data set to do so. However, we can still do a confusion matrix here. Notice in the data in the first row the predicted class does not agree with the data actual class. There is misclassification (a common occurrence with classification modelling).

	Predicted class 0	Predicted class 1
Actual class 0	5	0
Actual class 1	1	4

However, now let's use the model for classification and consider a scenario where we have new individuals with unknown adult or child status, but we do have their height data. Using the logistic regression model, we built earlier, we can input these height values to predict the probability of being an adult or a child.

Height, in	Adult_Binary	p pred	Predicted binary
60	1	0.310026	0
47	0	0.000142	0
36	0	1.55E-07	0
66	1	0.948826	1
61	0	0.455121	0
57	0	0.065375	0
72	1	0.998695	1
65	1	0.908877	1
60	0	0.310026	0
68	1	0.984632	1
50		0.000911	0
55		0.01984	0
60		0.310026	0
65		0.908877	1

New data and predictions

This prediction aspect is where classification models shine. By creating a model from existing data, we can then use it to predict outcomes for new data. For example, in financial settings, you might use historical loan default data to build a model that predicts whether new loan applicants are likely to default.

Graphically, logistic regression curves typically take on an S-shaped form. The y-axis represents the probability of belonging to a particular category.

As you move along the curve, you encounter the threshold where the probability is 50/50, indicating the boundary between the two categories. Any misclassification tends to occur around this midpoint.

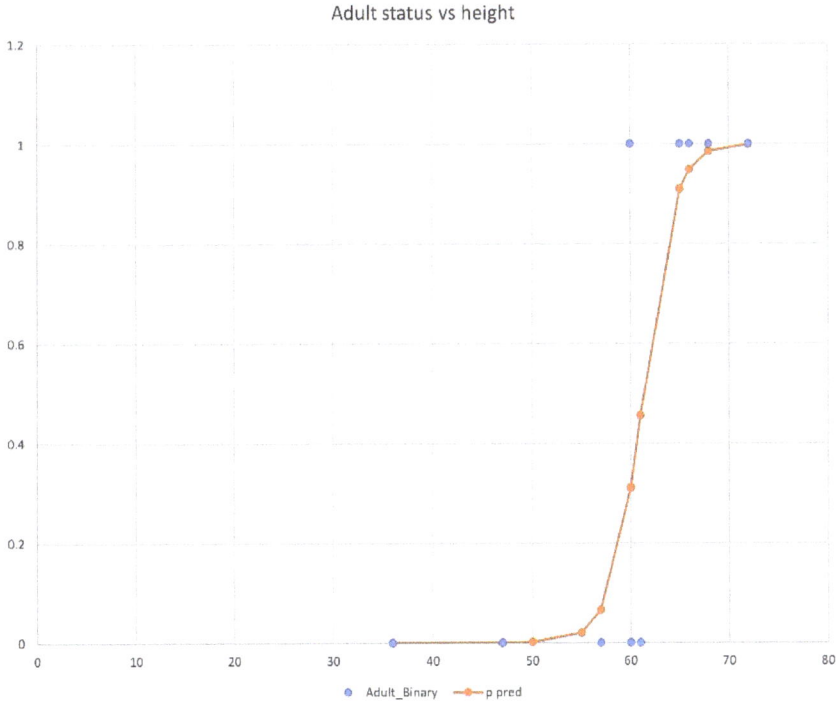

Adult status vs height

Now, let's discuss the possibility of using multiple predictors (the x variables or inputs). While we won't delve into making and using multiple regression here, it's an important concept. In our previous example, we only used height as the predictor variable of whether someone is an adult. However, in more complex models, you can include multiple factors like height, weight, and others.

Multiple regression: 2+ input variables

$$y = \beta_0 + \beta_1 x_1 + \beta_2 x_2 + \dots + \beta_n x_n$$

Logistic regression: 2+ input variable

$$\ln \frac{p}{1-p} = \beta_0 + \beta_1 x_1 + \beta_2 x_2 + \dots + \beta_n x_n$$

It's crucial to exercise caution when adding predictors. While some models may benefit from multiple inputs, you don't want to overcomplicate things. Generally, sticking to a few key predictors is advisable to keep the model manageable and interpretable. While technically you can add as many predictors as you want, it's essential to maintain a balance between complexity and practicality. In higher-level machine learning and artificial intelligence, models can indeed become much more complex. However, for practical applications of classification, simplicity is often key.

Additionally, logistic regression isn't limited to variables having binary outcomes already in the data. Through derived variables, you can create new binary outcomes based on your specific needs. Creating a binary outcome from categorical data is straightforward. Whether it's categorizing animals like cats, dogs, birds, or fish, you can easily translate this into a binary outcome of "dog" versus "not dog." This flexibility makes logistic regression and classification more versatile than it might seem at first glance.

Review Questions

1. What does logistic regression predict?
2. How is it different from linear regression?
3. What is a logit?
4. What is an odds ratio?
5. What does a probability of 0.8 mean in a model?
6. How do we turn probabilities into class labels?
7. What is a confusion matrix?
8. When would you use logistic regression in real life?
9. Why not add too many predictors?
10. What does the 0.5 threshold mean?

5-4 Decision trees

Learning Outcomes

5-4-1 Describe what a decision tree is and how it works.

5-4-2 Identify the parts of a decision tree (root, branches, leaf nodes).

5-4-3 List the pros and cons of using decision trees.

5-4-4 Explain what "impurity" means and how it affects splits.

5-4-5 Recognize when a tree is too complex (overfitting) and how to fix it.

5-4-6 Understand why it's important to test your tree on new data.

5-4-7 Use a confusion matrix to see how well your tree works.

As the name suggests, decision trees are a classification algorithm where classifying occurs in steps (tree levels) and work by recursively splitting the data based on certain criteria. This iterative process results in a tree-like structure where each node represents a decision based on a specific attribute or feature of the data.

One key advantage of decision trees is their simplicity—they don't require extensive data normalization or manipulation. Plus, they produce a visual representation that's easy to interpret, making them accessible even to those without advanced technical expertise. Another major benefit of decision trees is their versatility. Unlike some other methods, they can handle both numerical and categorical data without the need for complex calculations. However, they do have their drawbacks, notably in terms of computation time. The process of recursively splitting the data can be computationally intensive, especially for large datasets.

So, how does a decision tree work? It starts with the entire dataset and iteratively splits it into smaller subsets based on the values of different attributes. Each split is chosen to maximize the homogeneity or purity of the resulting subsets with respect to the target variable. This process continues until certain stopping criteria are met, such as reaching a maximum tree depth or achieving a minimum number of samples in each leaf node.

Imagine you have your dataset with various predictor variables, like X_1, X_2, X_3, and so on. The decision tree algorithm kicks off by determining which variable provides the best split for the data.

Now, each split must result in mutually exclusive categories—there can't be any overlap. For instance, you might have splits like "age less than 10" and "age greater than or equal to 10." This ensures clear delineation between the groups. The splitting process continues iteratively until a stopping criterion is met. This criterion is reached when there's no discernible reason to split the data further. Essentially, you keep splitting until there's nothing left to distinguish between the groups.

Visually, a decision tree resembles an upside-down tree, starting from a single root node and branching out into different decision nodes and leaf nodes. Each decision node represents a split based on a specific variable, while leaf nodes represent the outcome or prediction. At the top is what we call the root node. Moving down, we have internal nodes, which are like decision points within the tree. Finally, at the bottom are the leaf nodes, which are the final outcomes or predictions. These nodes have no children, meaning they're the end points of the tree.

With each split in a decision tree there's a chance of misclassification, which translates to the probability of encountering false positives or false negatives. However, in decision trees for looking at split accuracy, instead of referring to misclassification, we use the term "impurity." So, the goal with each split is to minimize impurity, essentially minimizing the misclassification rate, albeit termed differently. This is evaluated using a metric called the Gini index, which quantifies impurity. So, the aim at each step is to minimize both the Gini index and the misclassification rate, which are key metrics in decision tree analysis.

Now, let's take a closer look at an example. Here, we're classifying individuals based on whether they're considered senior citizens, with age being the only criterion. The tree shows a split based on age, dividing individuals into two groups: those at or under 51 and those over 51. The data is already sorted accordingly, with individuals falling into either category. The tree provides a visual representation of the distribution within each group. For instance, out of the eight individuals, five are not senior citizens, while three are.

Age	Senior citizen (>65)
4	N
15	N
22	N
16	N
51	N
66	Y
75	Y
80	Y

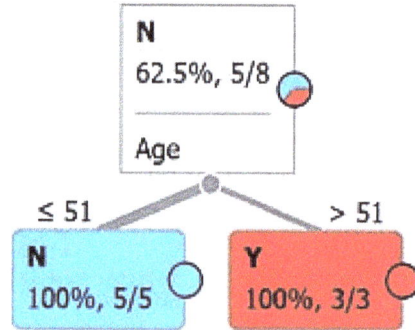

Overall, this decision tree simplifies the classification process by using a single variable—in this case, age—to make predictions. While this example is relatively straightforward, decision trees can become more complex when multiple variables are involved. Let's delve into another example to better understand decision trees. In this case, we're using three variables: age, dog ownership, and car driving. The goal is to predict whether someone drives a car based on these factors.

Age	Has dog	Drives car
4	N	N
15	Y	N
22	Y	Y
16	N	Y
51	Y	N
66	N	Y
75	N	Y
80	Y	Y

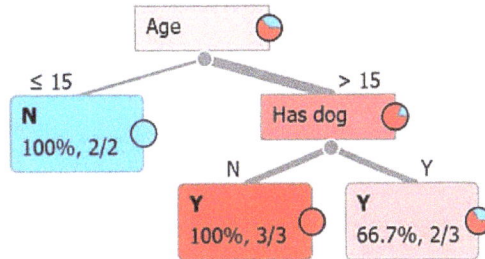

Starting at the top of the tree, we first split the data based on age. Individuals aged 15 or younger are categorized as "no" since they likely don't have a driver's license. Conversely, individuals older than 15 are more likely to drive, except for one person. Next, we further split the data for a second split based on dog ownership although note this split is largely noninformative for classifying car driving as it seems from this example dog ownership has little to do with driving.

It's crucial to note that having a subgroup (leaf node) with only one individual, as seen in the final split, indicates overfitting. This means the decision tree is too tailored to the specific data and may not generalize well to new data. The technique of pruning involves removing excessive branches from the decision tree to mitigate overfitting, which occurs when individual data points are overly accommodated. By specifying a minimum threshold for the number of data points in each group during the split, you can prevent the tree from becoming overfit. This minimum threshold ensures that each group maintains a sufficient sample size for reliable classification.

To assess the overall effectiveness of the decision tree, you need to determine the number of overall misclassifications, which is different from evaluating split impurity. Misclassifications occur at the end of the decision tree, where the predicted outcomes may not align with the actual classifications.

When evaluating the overall effectiveness of a decision tree, it's essential to split the data into training and testing sets. Testing against unseen data helps assess the tree's generalizability and effectiveness beyond the training data.

While decision trees offer a valuable tool, it's crucial to exercise caution and not overestimate their capabilities, especially in critical applications like disease outcome prediction. Decision trees are not overly sophisticated; they're more exploratory in nature. Additionally, comparing multiple trees using the same data can be beneficial. You can experiment with different tree configurations, such as pruning, to refine the model's performance. Often a simpler decision tree with fewer levels may be more suitable, as it reduces the risk of overfitting and yields better overall performance. Use confusion matrices to compare performance of various decision tree configurations and determine the optimal balance between complexity and accuracy.

Review Questions

1. What is a decision tree used for?
2. What are the three main parts of a decision tree?
3. Name one benefit and one drawback of decision trees.
4. What does "impurity" mean in a decision tree?
5. What is overfitting, and how can pruning help?
6. Why do we split data into training and testing sets?
7. What is a confusion matrix and why is it useful?
8. Why might a simple decision tree be better than a complex one?

5-5 K nearest neighbors

Learning Outcomes

5-5-1 Say what KNN is and what the "K" means.
5-5-2 Explain how KNN decides a class using nearby points.
5-5-3 Understand why we need to scale or standardize data first.
5-5-4 Pick a good number for K (like 3 or 5).
5-5-5 Describe how KNN uses a majority vote to decide.
5-5-6 Know that KNN uses distance to find close points.
5-5-7 Explain why too big a K isn't helpful.

K-nearest neighbors (KNN) is a classification algorithm that assigns observations to classes based on their proximity to nearby points. It determines classification by calculating the mathematical distance between points. The "K" in KNN refers to the number of neighboring points considered during this classification process.

KNN works best with a relatively small number of quantitative input variables. For accurate results, these input variables should all be on the same scale (e.g., all in inches, all in percentages) or normalized, as discussed earlier.

In many data mining algorithms, including clustering and classification methods like KNN, distances are crucial. To ensure that the scale of measurement does not unfairly influence the results, standardized scores are used. This concept was covered in a prior chapter.

Now, let's dive into K-nearest neighbors (KNN) using an example dataset on height and weight.

Height (in)	Weight (lb)	Adult (>16)
60	170	Y
47	85	N
36	54	N
66	175	Y
61	160	N
57	165	N
72	190	Y
65	145	Y
60	110	N
68	180	Y

Because weight values typically overshadow height due to their larger numerical range KNN should not be performed on the data until it is standardized. By standardizing, we level the playing field, ensuring that both height and weight contribute equally to classification decisions.

Height (in)	Weight (lb)	Adult (>
0.079	0.6188	Y
-1.209	-1.3585	N
-2.300	-2.0796	N
0.674	0.7351	Y
0.178	0.3861	N
-0.218	0.5025	N
1.269	1.0840	Y
0.575	0.0372	Y
0.079	-0.7769	N
0.872	0.8514	Y

In the scatterplot the x-axis represents height, while the y-axis denotes weight. Adults are marked in red, while children are blue. Looking at the plot, you'll notice distinct clusters for adults and children, with a transitional area in between.

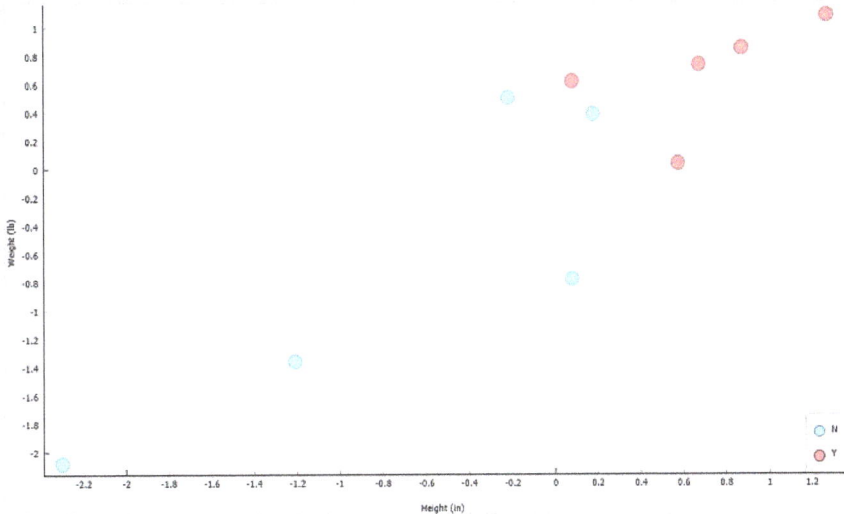

Imagine you have a new data point with known height and weight but an unknown classification, whether it's a child or an adult. We want to classify this new point based on its proximity to existing data points. K nearest neighbor uses k closest neighbors to new data and the new point is classified with the majority for the k nearest neighbors to determine the class of the new point. We introduce our new data point, represented as a dot with no assigned label.

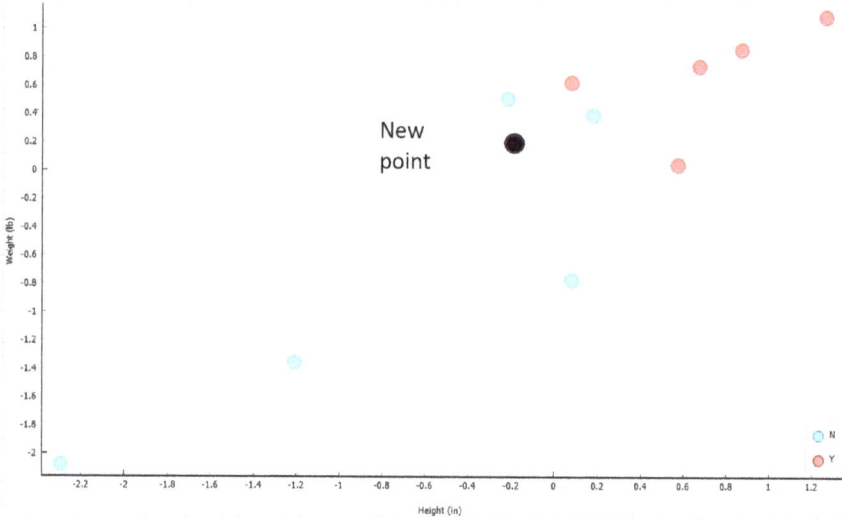

Now, the K in K-nearest neighbors represents the number of neighboring points we consider. A good choice would be to use k=3 closest neighbors (by standardized mathematical distance) to classify so we then identify the three nearest neighbors to our new point. If two of them are blue (representing children) and one is red (representing an adult), we classify our new point as blue, or a child. The KNN algorithm assigns the new data point to the majority class of the k neighboring points.

K=3

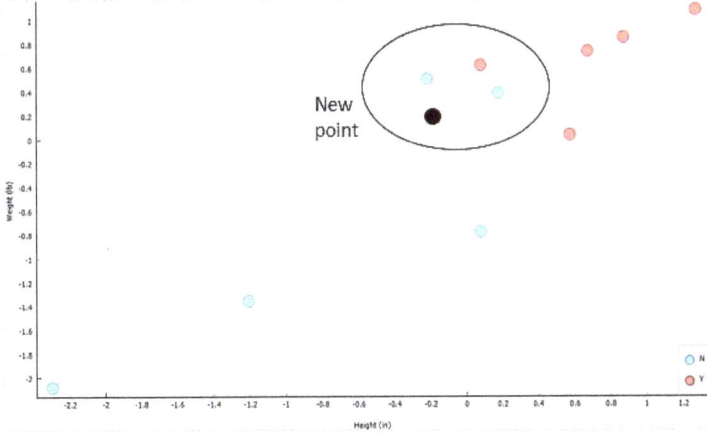

Another reasonable choice would be to use k=5 and consider the class of 5 nearest neighbors in assigning the new point its class. Here again blue is the majority class to which the new point is assigned.

K=5

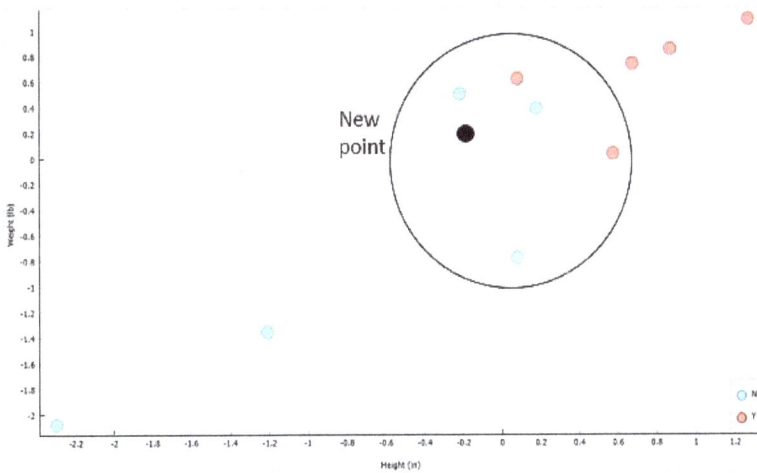

The exact choice of k is flexible (usually 3 or 5) but should be an odd number since an even number may result in an even split of neighbors with no majority class to assign a new point. Why? Because it could lead to a tie in classification. For instance, with two neighbors of each type, we'd face a 50/50 split, making it challenging to determine the correct classification. Therefore, odd values like three or five are preferred, ensuring a clear majority for classification.

In summary, K-nearest neighbors is a straightforward algorithm where classification is determined by the majority vote of the nearest neighbors. It's a handy tool for classification tasks, offering simplicity and effectiveness. It's also worth noting that K-nearest neighbors typically employs Euclidean distance as the default distance metric, although other options are available depending on the specific application.

Lastly, the value of K can technically range from one to the total number of data points. However, it's typically chosen based on the size of the dataset and the desired level of classification granularity. For instance, in a dataset with 10 data points, a value of K could range from one to 10, depending on the specific classification task at hand. You could technically set k = 10, but that would essentially be pointless because you'd be selecting the entire dataset. In such a case, you'd simply go with the majority class, rendering the classification meaningless. That's why three or five is typically the preferred choice for the number of neighbors used in K-nearest neighbors.

Review Questions

1. What does "K" mean in KNN?
2. How does KNN decide the class of a new point?
3. Why do we need to scale (standardize) the data in KNN?
4. Why is it better to use an odd number for K?
5. What kind of distance does KNN usually use?
6. What happens if K is too big?
7. Is KNN a simple or complex method?

5-6 Evaluating model performance

Learning Outcomes

5-6-1 Understand why model evaluation is essential in classification.

5-6-2 Explain the purpose of train/test splits and the need for randomization.

5-6-3 Interpret a confusion matrix and calculate accuracy.

5-6-4 Read and analyze ROC curves and AUC.

5-6-5 Understand how k-fold cross-validation improves evaluation.

Moving on to delve into the crucial topic of evaluating model performance in classification. This aspect is paramount because, while you can create a model, its effectiveness hinges on its ability to accurately classify data. Therefore, understanding how to assess the performance of your model is essential for ensuring its practical utility. Whether you're employing decision trees, logistic regression, or K-nearest neighbors, the approach to evaluating model performance remains consistent.

The first step in this evaluation process involves randomized splitting the data into training and testing sets. This step is fundamental and applies universally across various classification methods. By partitioning the data in this manner, you create a distinct subset for training the model and another for testing its performance. This enables you to assess how well your model generalizes to new, unseen data—a critical aspect of model evaluation.

Evaluating model performance is a fundamental aspect common to all classification methods. When developing a classification model, there may be various options to consider. For instance, if you're dealing with a binary outcome, you might want to explore both logistic regression and decision tree models for the same dataset to determine the most effective approach. It's important not to limit yourself to just one model type but rather to experiment with different ones and compare their performance metrics. Ultimately, the goal is to identify the model with the best predictive ability, which translates to the fewest misclassifications or the lowest misclassification rate.

The assignment of test and training data should be random to ensure unbiased evaluation. Avoid using sorted data for this purpose, as it can lead to skewed results. In tools like Excel, you can easily achieve random selection by using functions like RAND to shuffle the data before splitting it. However, in some software like R, achieving randomization from sorted data might be more challenging, so it's essential to find appropriate methods or libraries to handle this effectively. Remember, random sampling ensures that your test and training datasets are representative of the overall dataset and yield reliable evaluation results.

Once you have your training and test datasets, you'll compare the predicted outcomes with the actual outcomes in the test data. For instance, if the model predicts A but the actual outcome is B, it's a misclassification. Similarly, if the model predicts B but the actual outcome is A, it's another misclassification. Ideally, you'd want zero misclassifications, but that's rare in practice. Instead, you aim to minimize misclassifications by evaluating different models and choosing the one with the lowest misclassification rate.

Confusion matrix

Recall the misclassification table is officially known as a confusion matrix. In essence, the confusion matrix summarizes classification results. For instance, in the drug test example, a true positive occurs when a positive prediction matches a positive outcome. Conversely, a false positive arises when a positive prediction mismatches a negative true outcome. Likewise, a false negative occurs when a negative prediction mismatches a positive true outcome.

	Predicted class A	**Predicted class B**
Actual class A	True positive (TP)	False negative (FN)
Actual class B	False positive (FP)	True negative (TN)

Finally, true negatives and true positives denote correct predictions and is referred to as the true positive rate. Evaluating the true positive rate provides valuable insights into classification performance. Accuracy is the proportion of classifications that are not misclassification and is calculated as (TP + TN) / Total, offering a comprehensive measure of the model's correctness. In classification tasks, accuracy is typically the metric of interest unless specific metrics are required.

It is important to note here that confusion matrices need not be two by two since many classification models may have more than two outcome categories. The principal calculations of false positives, false negatives, true negatives and true positives remain the same.

	Predicted class A	Predicted class B	Predicted class C
Actual class A	20	10	5
Actual class B	5	65	10
Actual class C	15	20	50

There are more metrics available for in-depth analysis, but for now, let's focus on these fundamental ones.

ROC curve and AUC

A ROC curve is a visual representation of a model's accuracy. The x-axis represents the false positive rate, while the y-axis represents the true positive rate. The curve starts from the bottom left, where the false positive rate is 0 and the true positive rate is also 0 and extends towards the top right.

Now, ideally, you want the curve to hug the left border and rise sharply towards the top left corner. This indicates a low false positive rate and a high true positive rate, which are signs of a strong model. Conversely, if the curve is closer to the diagonal 50/50 line, it means the model's performance is no better than random chance. The curve shown has about 80% accuracy.

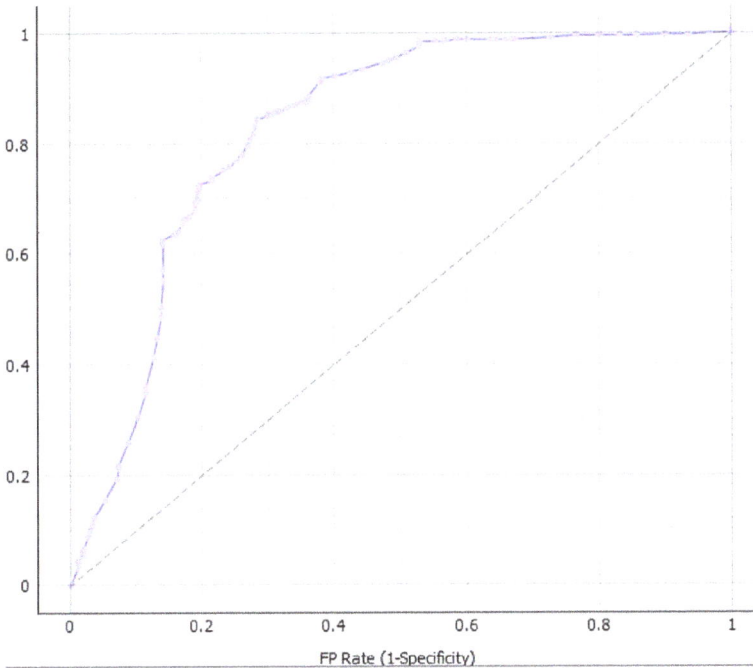

The area under the ROC curve (AUC) is a key metric. For a perfect model, the AUC would be 1, covering the entire area under the curve. In practical scenarios, a higher AUC indicates better model performance. So, when you see "AUC" as a model evaluation metric it refers to the area under this curve. The closer it is to 1, the better the model. Because ROC curves are visual and easy to interpret, they are a powerful tool for model evaluation.

K fold cross validation

Alright, let's delve into k-fold cross-validation. This method offers a more robust way to evaluate classification models, especially with larger datasets. Here's how it works. Instead of a single split into training and test sets, you divide your data into k parts or "folds." Typically, k is set to 10, but this can vary based on your dataset's size and complexity.

For each iteration, one-fold is held out as the test set, while the remaining k-1 folds are used for training. This process repeats k times, ensuring that each fold gets a chance to be the test set. After each run, you calculate your model's performance metrics, such as accuracy, precision, recall, etc., based on the test set's predictions. Finally, you aggregate the results from all k runs to get a comprehensive assessment of your model's performance. This approach provides a more reliable estimate of your model's accuracy by averaging the results over multiple iterations. It helps mitigate the variability that can arise from a single train-test split.

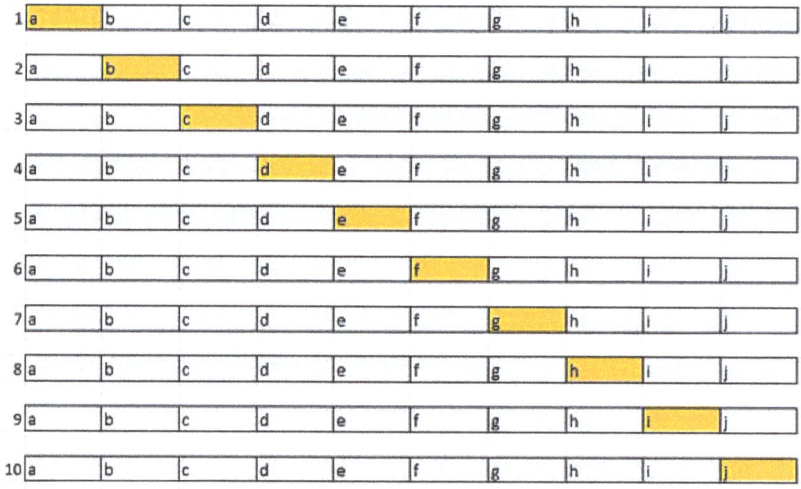

Review Questions

1. Why do we split data into training and testing sets?
2. What does a confusion matrix tell us?
3. How do you calculate accuracy from a confusion matrix?
4. What does a ROC curve show about model performance?
5. What is k-fold cross-validation and why use it?

Chapter 6

Association Analysis

6-1 Introduction

Learning Outcomes

6-1-1 Know what association analysis is and why it's useful.

6-1-2 Understand what an association rule is and what "A → B" means.

6-1-3 Explain why A and B in a rule must be different items.

6-1-4 Give examples of where association analysis is used, like in shopping or medicine.

6-1-5 Tell how this is different from clustering.

Association analysis delves into finding patterns among attributes or variables in a dataset. This data mining method falls under unsupervised learning. At its core are association rules, which define relationships between attributes in a dataset.

In simple terms, an association rule A →B consists of an antecedent (A) attribute and a consequent (B) attribute. The antecedent comes before the consequent. For instance, in a market setting, association rules can help determine if purchasing one product (A) is associated with purchasing another product (B) afterward. This insight is invaluable for marketing strategies.

It's crucial to note that the items involved (A and B) in association rules must be mutually exclusive. This means they don't share common elements. Items can be individual entities like "milk" and "butter," or they can form item sets, where multiple items are considered together.

Association analysis relies heavily on probability and aims to uncover meaningful relationships between items or item sets in a dataset. While it may not be as widely discussed as other data mining and machine learning techniques, its applications, especially in market analysis, are substantial.

Applications of association analysis

Association analysis, also known as affinity analysis or market basket analysis, is instrumental in examining patterns of items sold together. In sales and marketing analytics, understanding customer buying behaviors and identifying items that are frequently purchased together can have profound implications for marketing strategies and product placement. You might encounter this in everyday scenarios, like finding bananas strategically placed near peanut butter in grocery stores or receiving recommendations for complementary products while shopping online.

Beyond sales, association analysis can also have non-sales applications, such as identifying correlated symptoms to diagnose medical conditions or uncovering genetic patterns that co-occur. While it shares some similarities with cluster analysis, association analysis approaches these patterns differently, offering unique insights into data relationships.

Review Questions

1. What is association analysis used for?
2. What does the rule A → B mean?
3. Why must A and B in a rule be different items?
4. Can you give an example of how stores use association analysis?
5. How can this be used outside of shopping or sales?

6-2 Probability background

Learning Outcomes

6-2-1 Understand what probability is and how it's based on data.

6-2-2 Know how to calculate the chance of something happening.

6-2-3 Explain what a compound event is and how to find its probability.

6-2-4 Understand what conditional probability means.

6-2-5 Tell the difference between dependent and independent events.

Before delving into association rules, it's essential to grasp some basics of probability theory. Probability serves as the foundation for association rules, with probabilities derived from empirical data frequencies. For instance, if 100 items are sold, and 10 of them are coffee, the probability of selling coffee is calculated as 10 out of 100, or 0.10.

Probability theory extends beyond simple events like buying coffee to encompass compound events, where multiple occurrences are considered together. In association analysis, the focus shifts to these compound events, which can be broken down into simpler components. Let's explore the concept of compound events with an example: suppose in 10 shopping transactions, six involve the purchase of coffee (event A), four involve the purchase of ice cream (event B), and two involve the purchase of both coffee and ice cream. In this scenario, the probability of both A and B, purchasing both ice cream and coffee, occurring (denoted as A ⃞ B) is 2 out of 10.

Formally, in probability theory, compound events are often depicted using Venn diagrams. In this representation, the circles represent events A and B, with the overlapping region (purple in the diagram) indicating the occurrence of both events simultaneously. This is the joint probability.

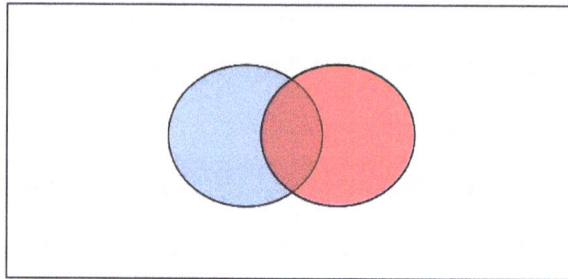

Conditional probability is another important concept, relating to events occurring in sequence. It considers the likelihood of event B happening given that event A has already occurred. For instance, if A represents the first purchase and B represents the subsequent purchase, conditional probability examines the probability of B occurring after A.

The probability of B given A (written $P(B|A)$) may or may not equal the probability of B alone. If event A influences the likelihood of event B, then the probability of B given A differs from the standalone probability of B. In such cases, the events are deemed dependent. For example, if A is smoking and B is developing lung cancer, the probability of lung cancer is affected by smoking, indicating dependency between the events. Conversely, if event A has no bearing on the probability of event B, then the events are considered independent.

The probability of B given A being equal to the probability of B signifies independence between the events. For instance, when tossing two coins sequentially, the outcome of the second coin toss is unaffected by the result of the first toss. Thus, the probability of getting a head on the second coin remains 0.5, regardless of the first toss, indicating independence between events.

Review Questions

1. What is probability, and how can we find it from data?
2. What is a compound event? Give an example.
3. What does it mean when we say "the probability of B given A"?
4. What are dependent events? Give an example.
5. What are independent events? How are they different from dependent ones?
6. If 2 out of 10 shoppers buy both coffee and ice cream, what is the probability of that happening?

6-3 Item set definition

Learning Outcomes

6-3-1 Know what an item set is.

6-3-2 Tell the difference between one-item, two-item, and three-item sets.

6-3-3 Understand that only *whether* an item was bought matters—not how many.

6-3-4 Give examples of item sets using simple cases like fruit.

Another fundamental concept is the notion of an item set in association analysis. An item set refers to a collection of one or more items frequently found together. These items can be actual physical objects, or any entity represented by discrete items. What's interesting is that an item set can comprise a single item or multiple items grouped together.

Consider a small fruit stand offering apples, bananas, and oranges. Customers can make purchases ranging from nothing to one, two, or all three items. In terms of item sets, each fruit—apple, banana, or orange—represents an individual item. Additionally, combinations of two items, such as apples and bananas, bananas and oranges, or apples and oranges, constitute two-item item sets. Similarly, a three-item item set signifies the purchase of all three fruits.

It's essential to note that item sets focus solely on whether a purchase occurred or not. The quantity bought—be it one, five, or ten—is irrelevant. The presence of an item in a transaction is what matters for association analysis, not its quantity.

Review Questions

1. Can an item set have just one item?
2. What is a two-item set? Give an example.
3. Why don't we care how many items were bought in association analysis?
4. List all the item sets possible using apples, bananas, and oranges.
5. If someone buys five bananas and one orange, what items are in the item set?

6-4 Association metrics

Learning Outcomes

6-4-1 Understand support, confidence, and lift.
6-4-2 Calculate and interpret these metrics.
6-4-3 Use them to identify useful patterns in data.

Now, let's delve into the three key metrics used in association analysis: support, confidence, and lift. Although they are computed using probability metrics, they have distinct nuances and are not just interpreted as probabilities.

Support

Support represents the proportion of total transactions containing a specific item or item set. For instance, if out of 20 transactions, six include butter, the support for butter is 6 out of 20, or 30%. Consider another example: if of 20 transactions two transactions include both milk and butter, the support for the item set "butter and milk" would be calculated as 2 out of 20 transactions or 0.1.

Support can be computed for individual items or combinations of items, known as item sets. It's essential to clarify the context when discussing an item set, as it can refer to joint purchases, such as "butter and milk," rather than individual items.

So, for a single item, the support equals its probability, while for a combination of items, the support signifies the probability of that specific combination occurring. For one antecedent (A) and no consequent, the one item case, support is just equal to P(A). For one antecedent (A) and consequent (B) support = P (A $\cap$ B), the joint probability. Recall from basic statistics, probability values can range from 0 to 1.

In practical terms support effectively quantifies the popularity or frequency of items, considering them as binary occurrences, regardless of quantity. It's akin to frequency but without accounting for total quantities, focusing solely on whether an item or item set appears or not. In essence, support measures how prevalent an item or item set is. This is useful for determining many things such as what products sell most.

Confidence

Moving on to confidence, it's essentially a form of conditional probability. Conditional probability P(B|A) is the probability of event B given event A has occurred. It gauges the likelihood of item B being purchased given that item A has been purchased. This metric operates within a restricted sample space defined by the occurrence of item A. Confidence, like support, ranges from 0 to 1, reflecting the probability scale's bounds—from impossibility (0) to certainty (1).

In Market Basket analysis, confidence quantifies the probability of purchasing item (or item set) B after item (or item set) A has been bought. The higher the confidence, the more likely the two items are sold together—a feature cherished by sales and marketing professionals. For instance, if out of 10 transactions, 5 involve apples, and out of those 5, 3 also include bananas, the confidence for the association rule "apple to bananas" would be 3 out of 5 or 60%. Mathematically expressed as P (Banana | Apple) = 3/5.

Similarly, for a two-item item set, such as apples and bananas, if out of 10 transactions, 5 involve apples, and out of those 5, 2 also include bananas and oranges, the confidence would be 2 out of 5 or 40%, reflecting the probability of purchasing bananas and oranges after buying apples. Mathematically P (Bananas, Oranges) | Apple) = 2/5 =0.4.

Lift

Lift measures how many times more likely it is to find the consequent item set (in this case, soda) when the antecedent item (chips) is present compared to when it's absent. Ex: if a person buys eggs (consequent B) how much more likely is it that they have purchased milk (antecedent A) than if they did not purchase milk.

As part of the lift measure, we need to introduce another concept, that of expected confidence. For A →B expected confidence is simply the probability of the consequent B. Ex: if there are 100 transactions, 40 involving chips, 20 involving soda, and 32 involving chips and soda. The expected confidence of soda is 20/100 or 0.2. For the association rule chips → soda. The confidence of soda is P (soda | chips) = 32/40 = 0.8.

Lift is calculated as the ratio of confidence to expected confidence. Note is a ratio of probabilities and is not constrained to 0 to 1 because of this. The Lift, for this example with the consequent being soda (B) and the antecedent being chips (A), is confidence/expected confidence = 0.8/0.2 = 4. This means that buying chips is 4 times more likely to occur with buying soda than without buying soda

Lift measures how much more likely the consequent B is to occur with the antecedent A having occurred than without. The higher the lift value the stronger the association of A and B. This ratio of probabilities provides insight into the strength of the association between items. A lift value greater than 1 indicates that the consequent item set is more likely to be bought when the antecedent item is purchased, suggesting a positive association. Conversely, a lift value less than 1 suggests a negative association, meaning that the presence of the antecedent item reduces the likelihood of purchasing the consequent item set. If the lift is exactly 1, it implies that there is no association between the antecedent and consequent items. This metric helps businesses identify significant item associations and optimize product placement or marketing strategies accordingly.

Review Questions

1. What does support show us in association analysis?
2. If an item appears in 6 out of 30 transactions, what's its support?
3. If 4 out of 10 milk buyers also buy eggs, what's the confidence for milk → eggs?
4. What does lift measure?
5. What's the lift if $P(\text{soda}) = 0.25$ and $P(\text{soda} \mid \text{chips}) = 0.75$?
6. What does lift mean if it's: Less than 1? 1? Greater than 1?
7. Why look at all three metrics (support, confidence, lift)?
8. Give an example of two items often bought together.

6-5 Transactional data

Learning Outcomes

6-5-1 Understand what transactional data is.

6-5-2 Recognize what transaction data looks like.

6-5-3 Explain how to turn raw data into a table with one column per item.

6-5-4 Know why we use 1s (and usually not 0s) in association analysis.

6-5-5 Understand that the amount of an item bought doesn't change the analysis.

Data us in association analysis is considered 'transactional' data and may be set up as such. Essentially data will look like sales records:

Transaction ID	Items
1001	{A, B, C}
1002	{B, C, D, E}
1003	{A, C, D}
1004	{A, D, E}
1005	{B, C}

Typically, transactional data need (depending on software) to be reformatted as a traditional structured data table to be used for association analysis. After a bit of data wrangling the data should have a one column per item structure with one row per transaction and binary flags for whether the item was purchased.

Transaction ID	A	B	C	D	E
1001	1	1	1		
1002		1	1	1	1
1003	1		1	1	
1004	1			1	1
1005		1	1		

Note the lack of fill in 0's in the data. Including 0's makes the 0's part of the itemset analysis (so apple=1 and apple=0 are both included for purchased apple and not purchased apple) making the analysis more complex although occasionally this may be of interest.

Transaction ID	A	B	C	D	E
1001	1		1		0
1002	0		1		1
1003	1				0
1004	1	0		1	1
1005	0				0

Note that antecedent and consequent are arbitrary and can be interchanged depending on context and column order doesn't matter to the software. Also, multiple quantities of items don't matter (6 apples or 1 apple purchased are apple=1 for data purposes) as association analysis considers only the yes/no of an item purchased without regard for quantity purchased.

Review Questions

1. What does transactional data usually look like in sales records?
2. How do we change transaction data so it works for association analysis?
3. Why do we usually leave out the 0s when making the data table?
4. What does it mean when a column for an item has a 1 in it?
5. Why don't we include how many of each item someone bought?
6. What are antecedents and consequents in association analysis, and why doesn't their order matter?

6-6 Association analysis example

Let's put the concepts presented here into context with an example. Association analysis uses the association rule A →B where A and B are mutually exclusive (contain no common elements) to analyze the relational patterns between A and B. A and B are item sets. Support, confidence and lift are the quantitative metrics of association

Consider a simple case of 10 transactions and two items – milk and butter. A customer can purchase milk alone, butter alone or both milk and butter (If the customer purchases nothing than no transaction has occurred so no analysis).

Transaction	Milk	Butter
1	1	
2	1	
3		1
4		1
5	1	1
6		1
7	1	
8	1	1
9		
10		1

For this data there are two possible association rules to consider, for the antecedent and consequent in each the item set is a single item (milk or butter).

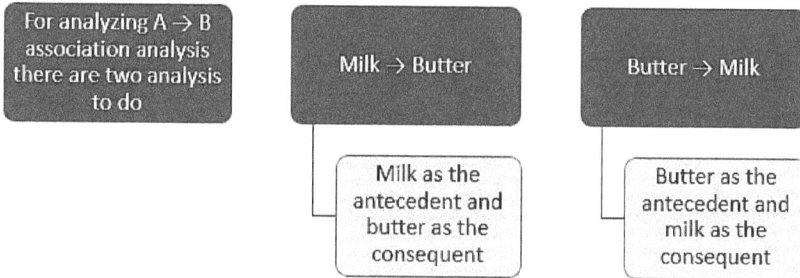

Now, let's dive into the calculations for the association metrics.

Let's start with support, which measures the frequency of occurrence of an item or item set in the dataset. Support is the proportion of the total transactions that contain that item or itemset. For milk the support is 5/10=0.5 since 5 of the 10 transactions include milk. The support for butter is 6/10 = 0.6. The support for the itemset of the two items milk and butter together is 2/10 = 0.2 (two of the 10 transactions purchase both).

Next, we'll explore confidence, which indicates the likelihood of buying one item given the purchase of another. Here, we're interested in the confidence of buying butter given the purchase of milk (Milk → Butter), and vice versa (Butter → Milk). These will have separate values for confidence as it is a conditional probability and inverse are usually not equal (occasionally by coincidence they are equal).

The confidence for Milk → Butter is the probability butter is purchased (consequent) GIVEN milk has been purchased (antecedent) and is P(Butter|Milk) = 2/5 =0.4.

The confidence for Butter → Milk is the probability milk is purchased (consequent) GIVEN butter has been purchased (antecedent) and is P(Milk|Butter) = 2/6 =0.33.

Finally, we'll examine the lift, which measures the strength of association between two items. A lift value greater than 1 indicates that the items are more likely to be bought together than separately.

For Milk → Butter, the confidence for this rule =0.4. The expected confidence of butter= 0.6. Lift = confidence/expected confidence =0.66. For Butter → Milk, the confidence for this rule =0.33. The expected confidence of milk = 0.5. Lift = confidence/expected confidence =0.66. In this example the lift is 0.66 for both association rules. The purchase of butter and milk are not strongly associated.

If we expanded the dataset to include apples, milk, and butter, the number of potential association rules would increase significantly. We must consider all permutations of one-item and two-item item sets, resulting in 12 different possibilities. Each combination requires calculation of support, confidence, and lift to understand the association between the item set.

Transaction	Milk	Butter	Apples
1	1		
2	1		
3		1	
4		1	1
5	1	1	1
6		1	1
7	1		
8	1	1	1
9			
10		1	

This expansion showcases the complexity that arises when dealing with larger datasets and multiple items. While the individual calculations may not be overly difficult, the sheer number of permutations can make manual computation impractical. This is where data analysis software becomes indispensable, allowing analysts to navigate through the multitude of association rules effectively.

When you view the output in software, you'll notice that the support column provides the frequency of occurrence for each combination of items. Support values for each item individually are in another section of the output.

Antecedent	Consequent	Support	Confidence	Lift
Apples=1	Butter=1	0.4	1	1.667
Butter=1	Apples=1	0.4	0.667	1.667
Butter=1	Milk=1	0.2	0.333	0.667
Milk=1	Butter=1	0.2	0.4	0.667
Apples=1	Milk=1	0.2	0.5	1
Milk=1	Apples=1	0.2	0.4	1
Butter=1, Apples=1	Milk=1	0.2	0.5	1
Milk=1, Apples=1	Butter=1	0.2	1	1.667
Apples=1	Milk=1, Butter=1	0.2	0.5	2.5
Milk=1, Butter=1	Apples=1	0.2	1	2.5
Butter=1	Milk=1, Apples=1	0.2	0.333	1.667
Milk=1	Butter=1, Apples=1	0.2	0.4	1

The support values are calculated based on the proportion of transactions that contain the specific combination of items. For the association rules the highest support is 0.4 for the itemset of apple and butter – this means this is the most popular two itemset sold.

Confidence, on the other hand, measures the likelihood of purchasing one item given that another item has been purchased. It's important to note that confidence is not commutative. The probability of buying item B given item A is not the same as the probability of buying item A given item B. This is why you'll see different confidence values for "butter given apples" and "apples given butter." The association rule BUTTER → APPLE has a confidence of 1.

This is because (look back to data) everyone who bought an apple had also purchased butter.

The lift ratios are another important metric in association analysis. The lift value indicates the strength of association between two items. Higher lift values suggest a stronger association. For instance, if the lift value for "apples given butter and milk", 2.5, is the highest among all combinations, it implies that purchasing apples is most strongly associated with purchasing butter and milk together.

These metrics provide different perspectives on association and can be used in combination to gain a comprehensive understanding of consumer behavior. For instance, while an item may not be very popular (low support), it could still have a high confidence if it's strongly associated with another item. This nuanced understanding allows marketers to tailor their strategies effectively.

Finally, let's consider practical applications like Market Basket analysis, which is highly relevant in sales and marketing. Understanding associations between products can inform strategies for product placement, promotions, and bundling, making it a valuable tool for business students, especially those specializing in marketing or sales analytics. Professionals in fields like sales and marketing specialize in analyzing buying behavior and devising selling strategies. This ultimately aims to boost revenue for themselves or their companies, which is the primary objective of business operations.

In healthcare, association analysis can be applied to identify patterns in symptoms that often co-occur, potentially aiding in disease diagnosis or treatment planning. For example, certain symptoms might be associated with specific medical conditions, helping healthcare professionals make more informed decisions. Understanding and working with association analysis is not overly complex either, making it accessible to a wide range of users.

www.ingramcontent.com/pod-product-compliance
Lightning Source LLC
Chambersburg PA
CBHW051859210326
41597CB00033B/5960